Chameleon Press

Kansas City, MO

Copyright 2020. Hugh Merrill

ISBN: 978-0-578-76099-5

Editor: Jeanette Powers

Cover art: Hugh Merrill

Designer: Aimée Harting

Photographer: Debbie Barrett-Jones

chameleonpress.com

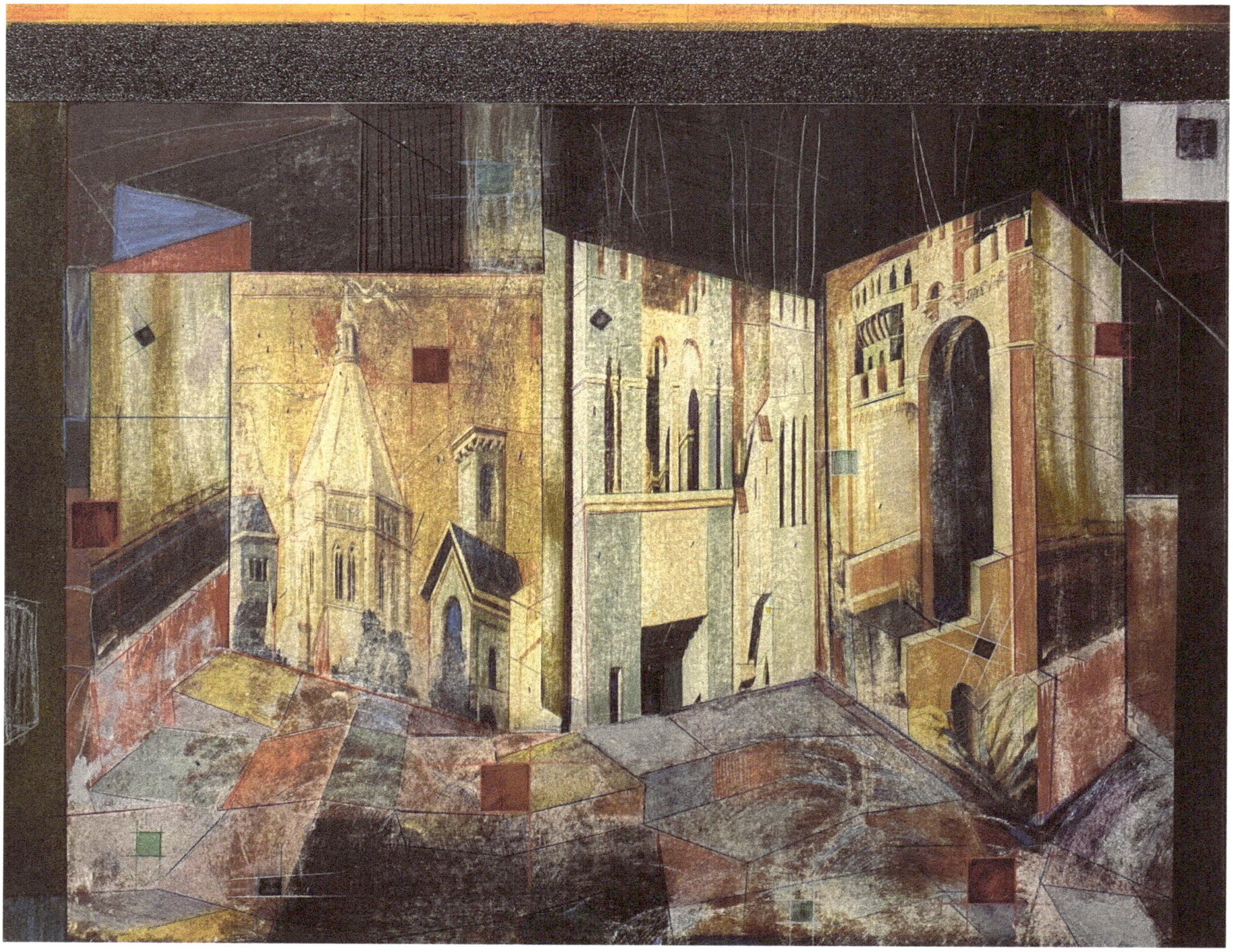

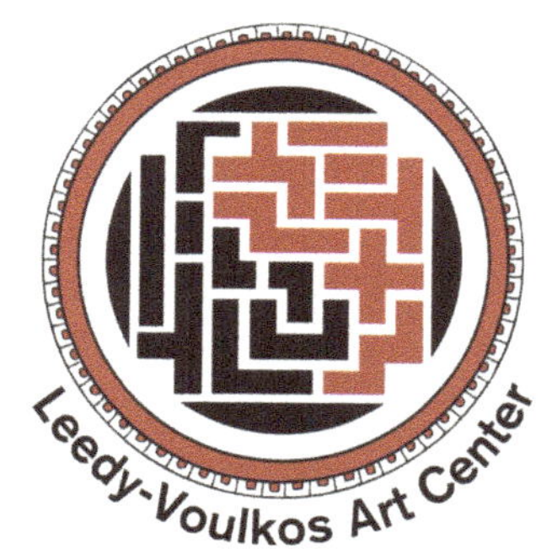

Making and Collaboration

Hugh Merrill and Jeanette Powers

2019-2020

2012 Baltimore Ave. KC MO 64108
www.leedy-voulkos.com   816-474-1919

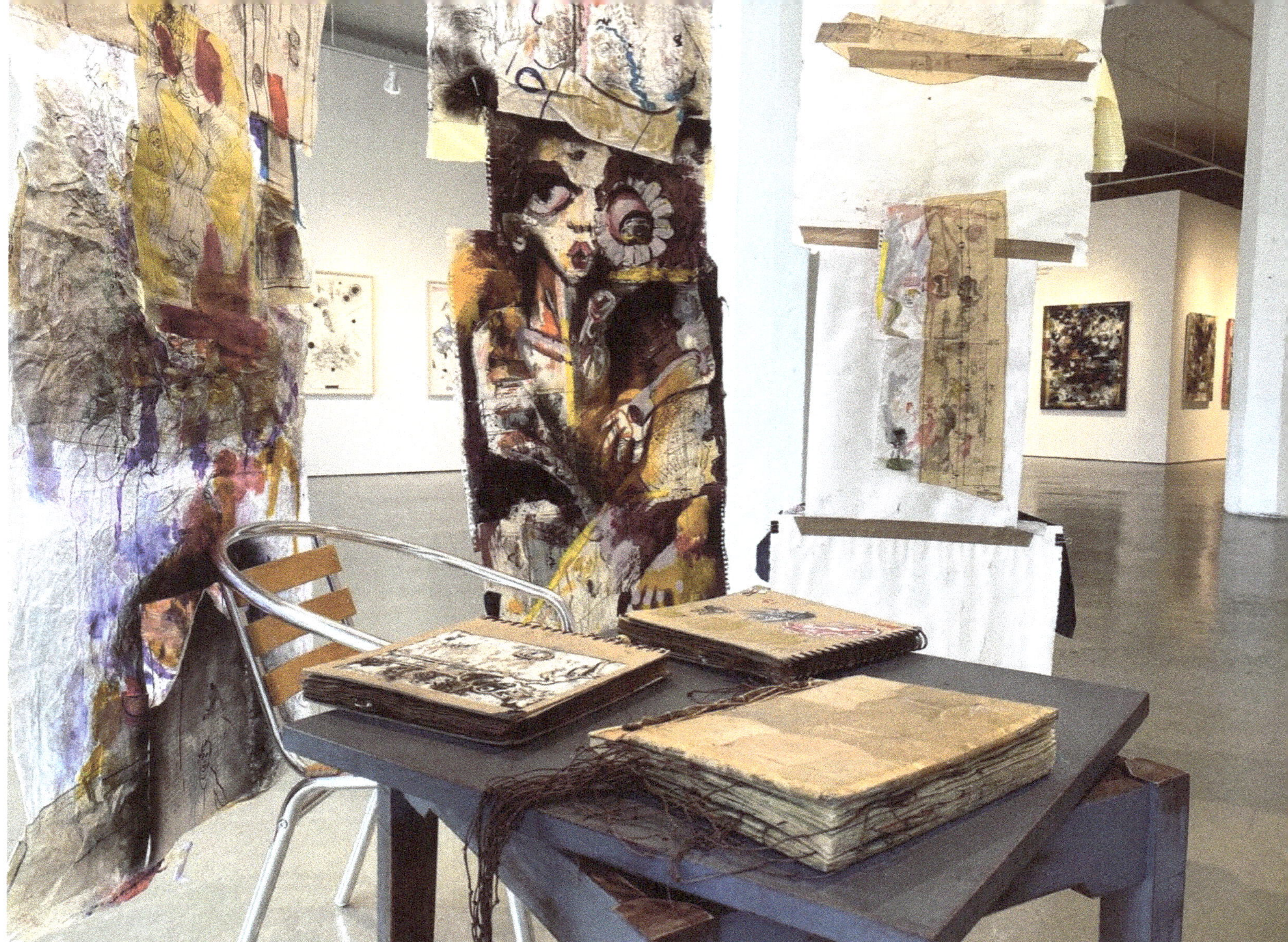

"The Interior Lives of Rabbits is an installation piece created over the summer of 2019 by Jeanette Powers and Hugh Merrill. The artists collaborated in dialogue first by challenging each other's repressions and dissociation to create a work which is, for the audience, both difficult to engage with emotionally and inviting a viewer to hold space for the emotional reactions.

The 'tent' panels are double-sided, as we are all more than the surface reveals, and create a barrier to space within the tent. They are made of reclaimed drop cloths, clothing scraps and Merrill's discarded sketchbook pages which have been taped, sewn, glued together in haphazard forms as a reflection of the patchwork way in which we reconfigure ourselves after the crisis, trauma, and the everyday cruelties of simply being in the world.

If a viewer chooses to enter the tent, however, space opens up of safety, comfort and invitation to deeper intimacy of the emotional space with the private, hand made one of a kind art books by Jeanette Powers. Each of the books addresses a different theme: Ennui faces suicidal ideations, Sage is a love letter to womanhood as Powers came out as non-binary, and finally, Dive is an exploration of when Powers had dissociated to the extreme of believing they were actually deceased.

The audience is given seats and a table in which to relax in the tent within the gallery setting, the 'barrier' transforms into a nest which establishes privacy and isolation for the human engaging with the art. Most significantly, the viewer is invited to touch, hold, engage with, read through Powers' art books, typically something forbidden in the art world due to potential damage to the art. In this space of full emotional availability through the vulnerable act of giving art to the fingers and touch of the audience, Merrill and Powers believe this to be an emblem of catharsis."

Over the past year, I have worked in a progressive, sequential manner in my studio. Moving from drawings on large sheets of paper with micron pens to works on birch panels. These solitary studio actions were counterbalanced by my collaborations with Jeanette Powers. For over three years we have collaborated on my memoir Whiteout, and in 2019 she edited and created graphics from my drawings for Dog Alley my second book of Poetry. We expanded our collaboration when we decided to exhibit Jeanette's visual journals as a major component of the exhibition 2019-2020. We meant every Wednesday night, for about 6 months, to produce double-sided hanging drawings/collages "as curtains" to create a sacred viewing space for her journals. I used graphics from the Whiteout project printed on sheets of Kozo as well as creating pen and ink drawings based on George Groz's Ecce Homo as the image resources for the drawings. When the curtains had been completed and prepared for hanging, I continued to make works related to Ecce Homo and the graphic illustration of my memoir. These works will be remade a third time in collaboration with acePIAR -the International Arts in Buenos Aires, Argentina June 2020.

Whiteout is conceived as a multi-dimensional project designed to create dialogues on heritage, privilege, power, and racism in America. It began with the publication of my memoir by Spartan Press. A memoir about growing up in a powerful political southern family. It has led to performance including staged readings from the memoir, a panel discussion, poetry audience participation. The first performance was held at Unity Temple on the Plaza on December 10th, 2019. Upcoming performances are being scheduled.

Whiteout, the Memoir "Over generations, my family helped shape the Jim Crow laws in Alabama,

convicted the innocent and saved the guilty. My Grandfather was the state judge in the trail that leads to the legal lynching of Sargent Edgar Caldwell in 1919. My uncle Hugh D. Merrill was George Wallace's whip in the State House in Alabama and defended the KKK that burned the freedom rider's bus in Anniston Alabama. My cousin is Secretary of State and presently running for the United States Senate seat from Alabama.

"Merrill, an internationally renowned artist, has written a memoir of his coming-of-age story in a house governed by those who helped write the Jim Crow laws, and the memoir is available now from Spartan Press." Jeanette Powers

The next phase of the project is to connect the stories and content to my ongoing studio work. I have been invited to The acePIAR/International Artist in Residence Program in Buenos Aires to produce a series of digital prints, drawings, monotypes on Mulberry Kozo paper 55x30 inches. 20 images are envisioned in the series. The series of works will be installed for the exhibition at Ace in July 2020.

Jeanette describes our work together on the Whiteout memoir "I have been fortunate to have been able to work with Merrill since the inception of this important project which focuses on race relations in America. Merrill grew up in a powerful, politically connected family in the Jim Crow South, and experienced firsthand much of the racial terrorism perpetrated by whites on people of color, even by folks in Merrill's own family. Merrill has focused on this project for over three years now and it has blossomed from a few small collages to a memoir, to a community engaging performative investigation of white privilege and fragility, and the exploration is now set to continue internationally, with a new series of paintings, and with other marginalized groups of folks. The overall mission of the Whiteout project is to create spaces for people to honestly share their experiences of racism and to work towards a society of justice and equity."

Artist Bio

Hugh Merrill is an artist/educator, writer and community activists. In 1985 he had a one-person exhibition at the Nelson Atkins Museum, and his work is in the collections of over 50 major museums such as the Museum of Modern Art New York, Kemper Museum KC, Cranbrook Museum and the National Museum of Poznan Poland. In 1996 he collaborated with French artist Christian Boltanski on the city-wide community arts project Our City Ourselves for the Kemper Museum. He was the past president of the Southern Graphics Council International and is a long-time professor at the Kansas City Art Institute. He developed Chameleon Arts and Youth Development into a resource for disenfranchised youth communities providing over 1 million dollars in community arts and youth development programming in the past 20 years. Merrill was selected as one of 42 international artists for Richard Noyce's book Printmaking At the Edge published in 2006. He has been awarded grants including 2 NEA grants, Melon Foundation, a Yaddo Fellowship, and the Distinguished Education Award from the Southern Graphics Council International 2007. In 2008 he was invited by the Nelson Atkins Museum to curate Print Lovers at Thirty. In September of 2009 his retrospective Divergent Consistencies, was exhibited by the Leedy-Voulkos Art Center. He has written Divergent Consistencies: 40 years of studio and community artwork, Shared Visions: Thoughts and Experiences in Social Arts Practice, Preaching to the Choir: thoughts on contemporary printmaking. His book of poetry Nomadic, was published by 39 West Press 2016 and the zine Whiteout: Journey of Privilege 2018 was recently completed. He is working with Missourians for Alternatives to the Death Penalty, the NAACP and the Black Archives of Kansas City to secure soil from Missouri's 60 lynching sites and send the jars of soil to the Equal Justice Initiative's Memorial for Peace and Justice.

Stream Series

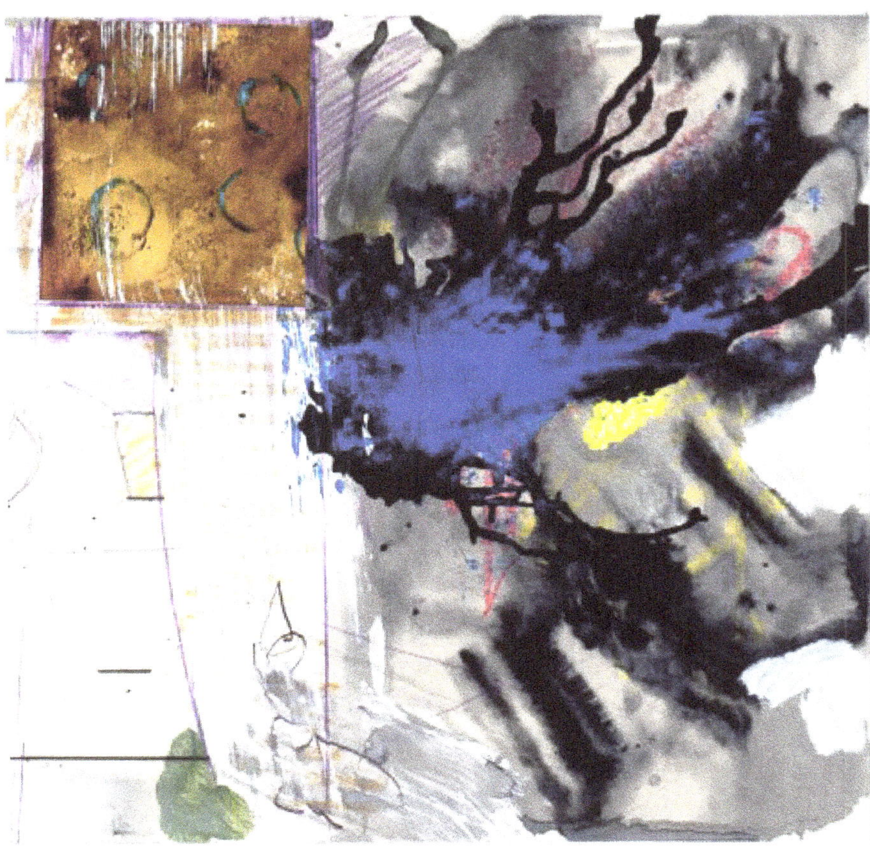

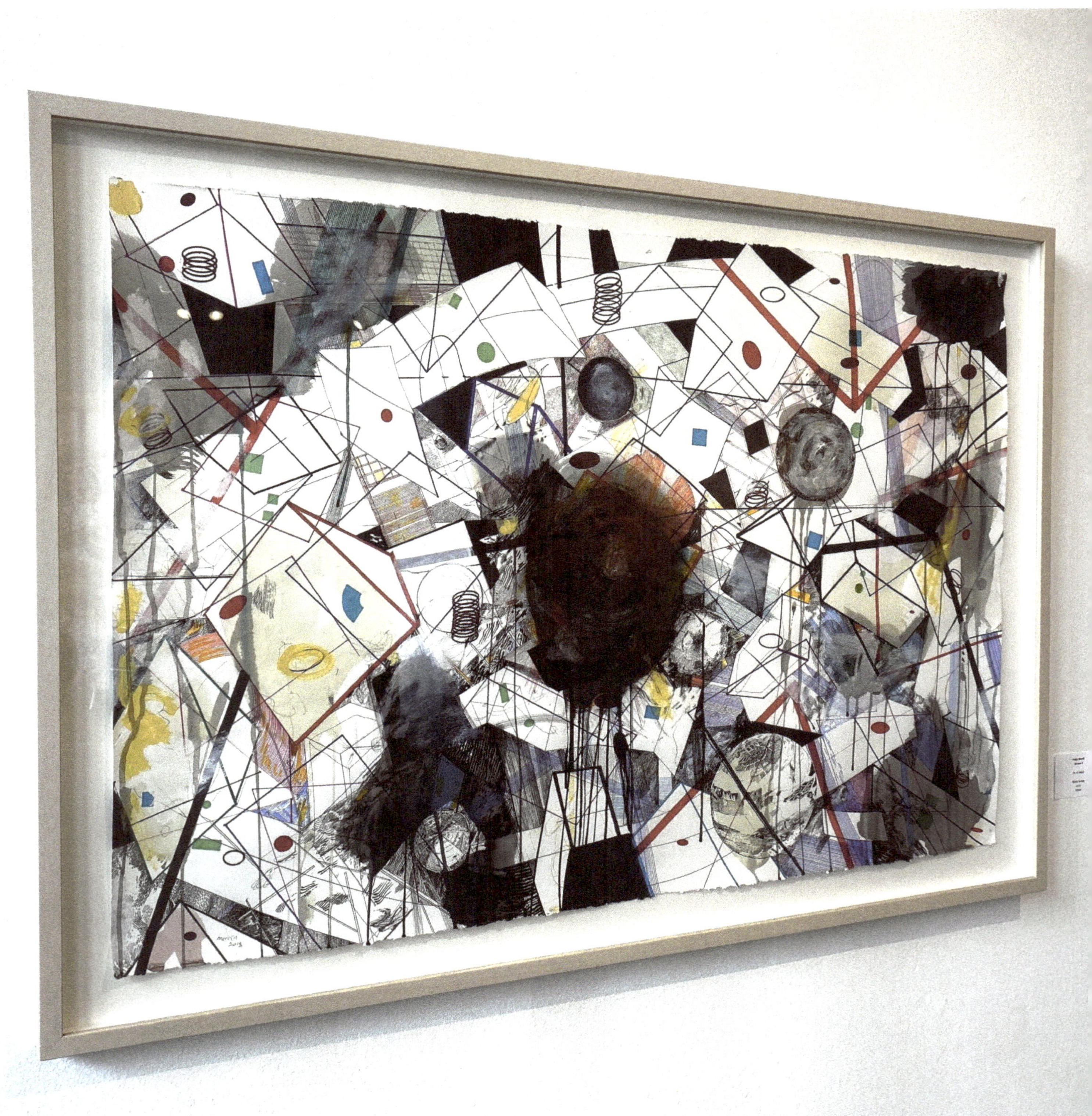

Stream 3
Ink on paper
30 x 44"
2019

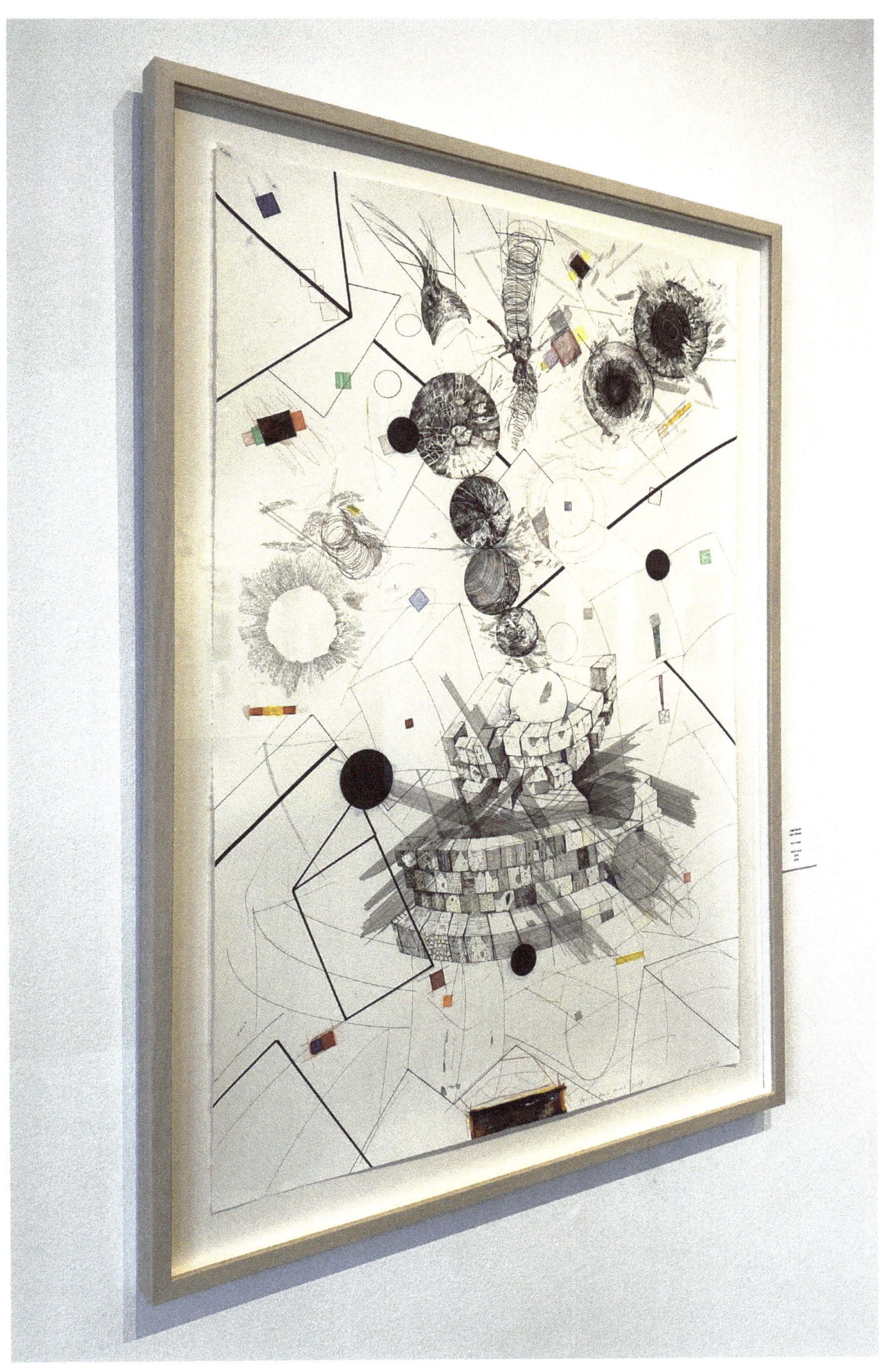

Erin's Stream
Ink on paper
44 x 30"
2019

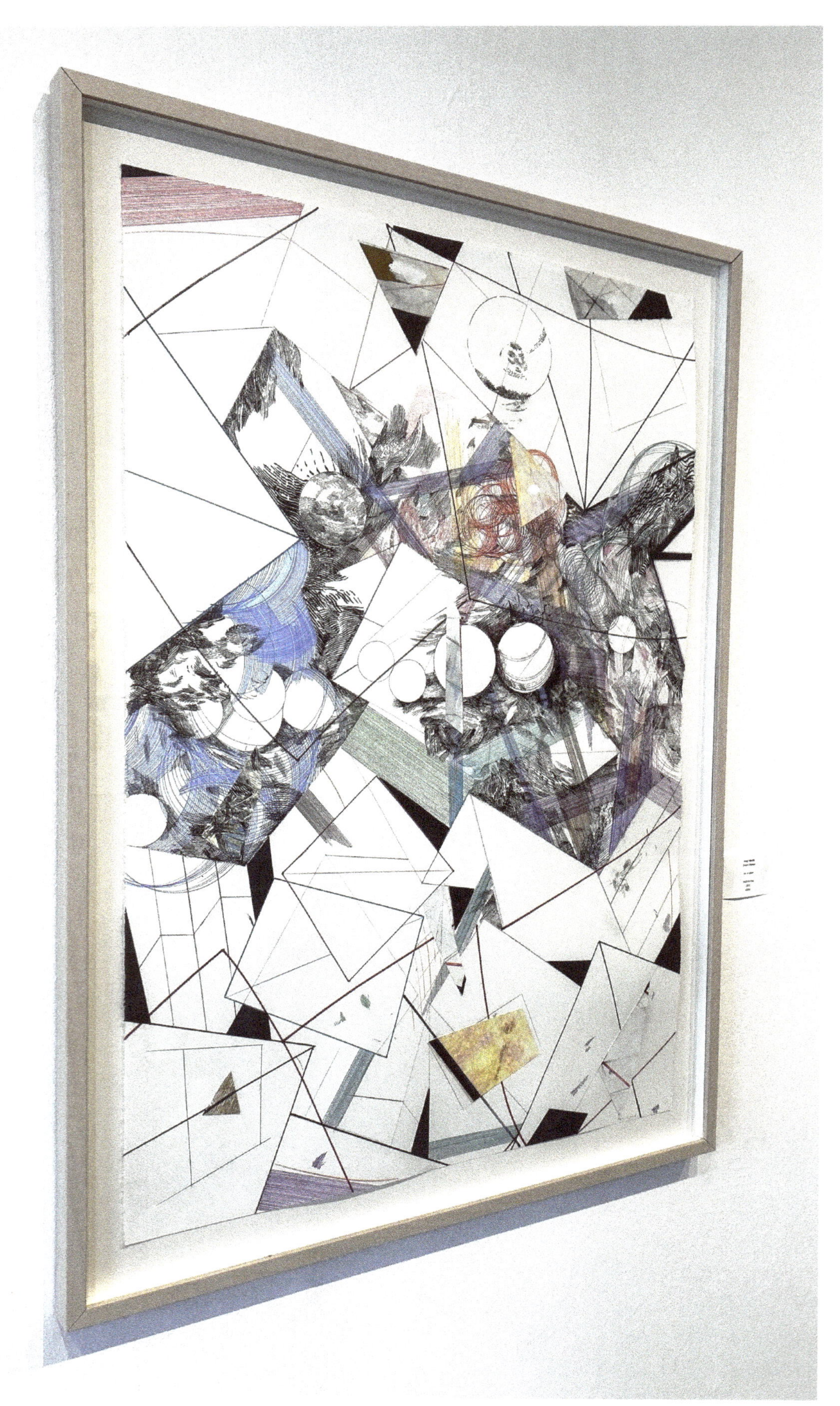

Cora's Stream
Ink on paper
44 x 30"
2018

Jacob's Stream   →
Ink on paper
44 x 30"
2018

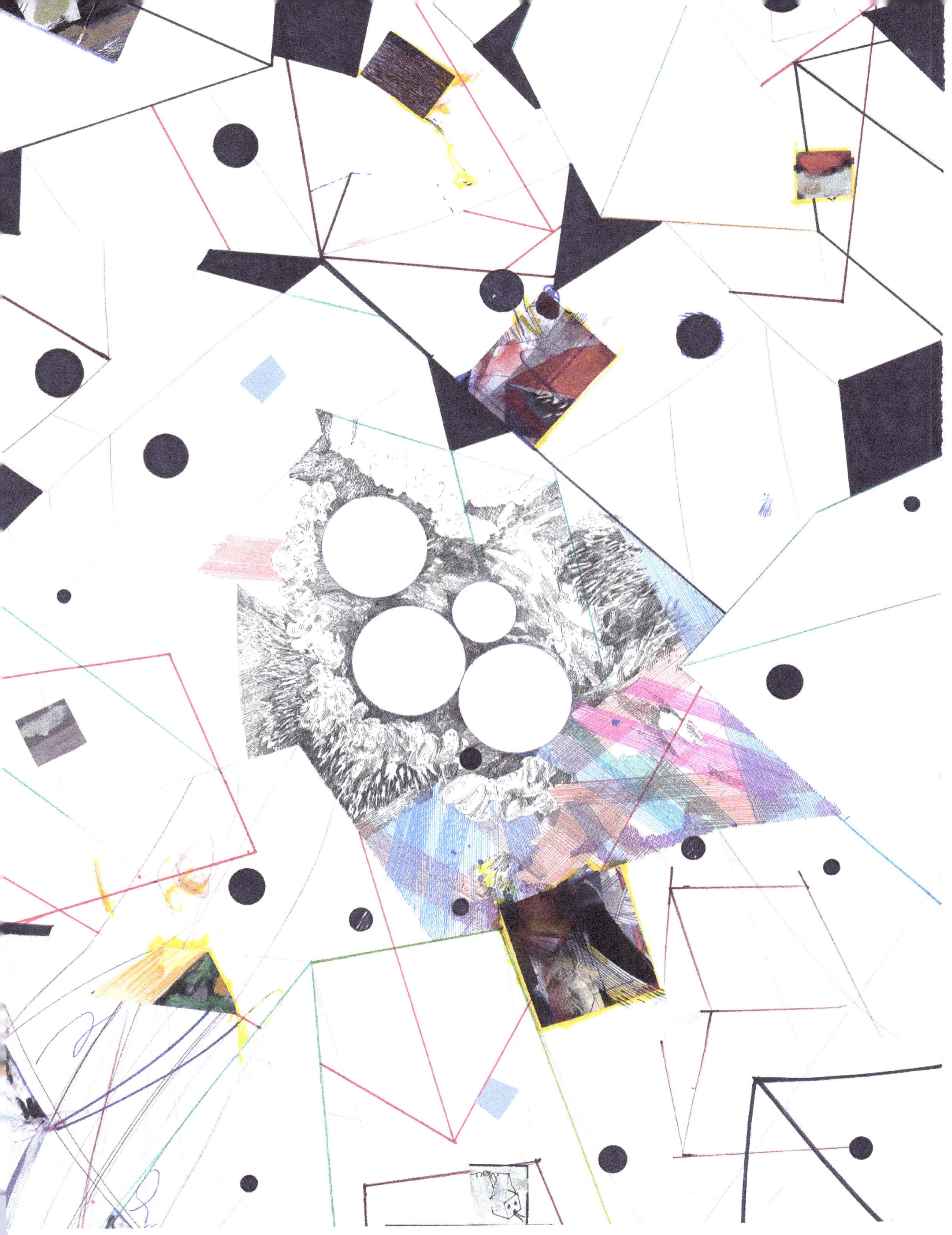

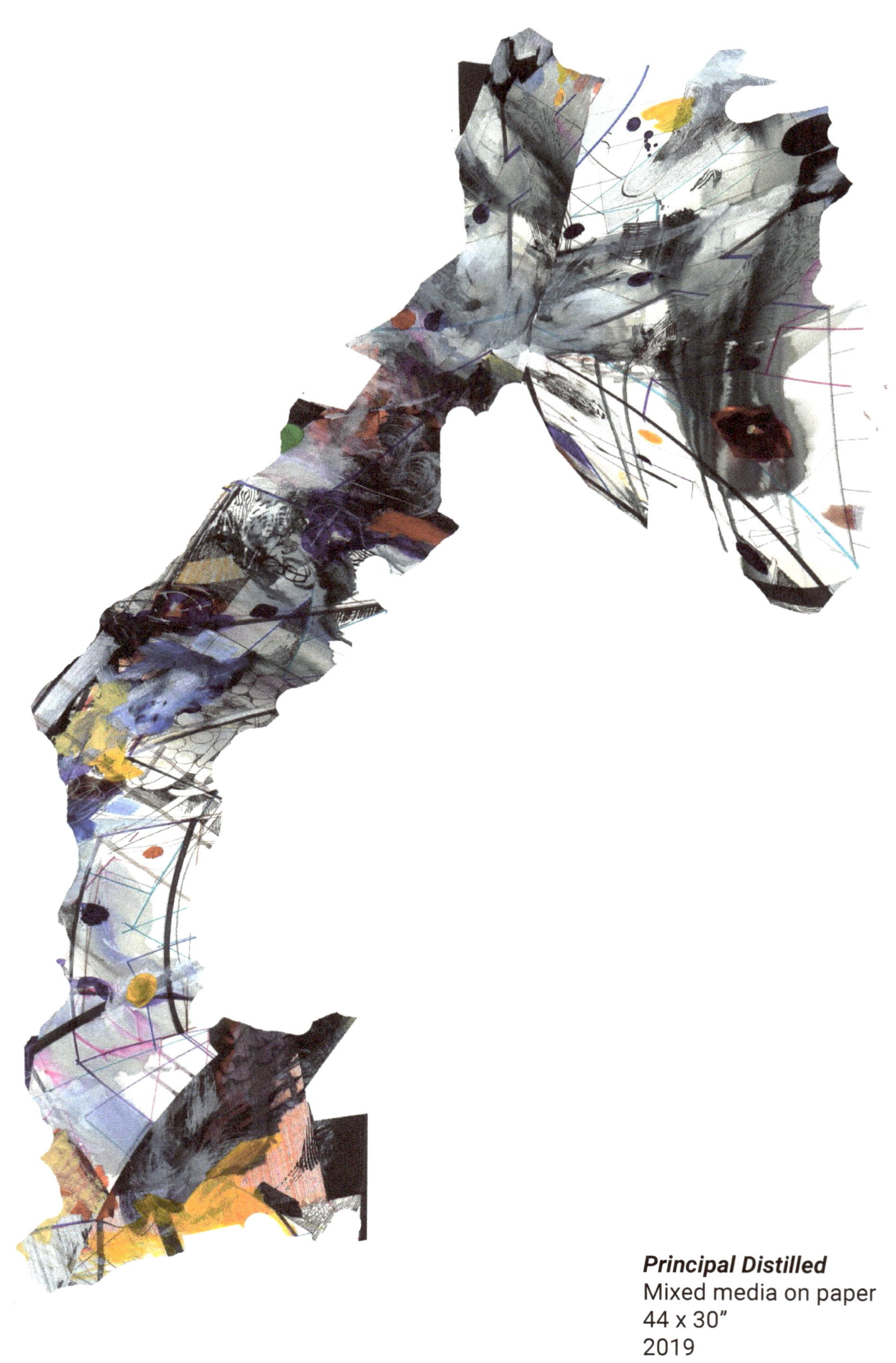

Principal Distilled
Mixed media on paper
44 x 30"
2019

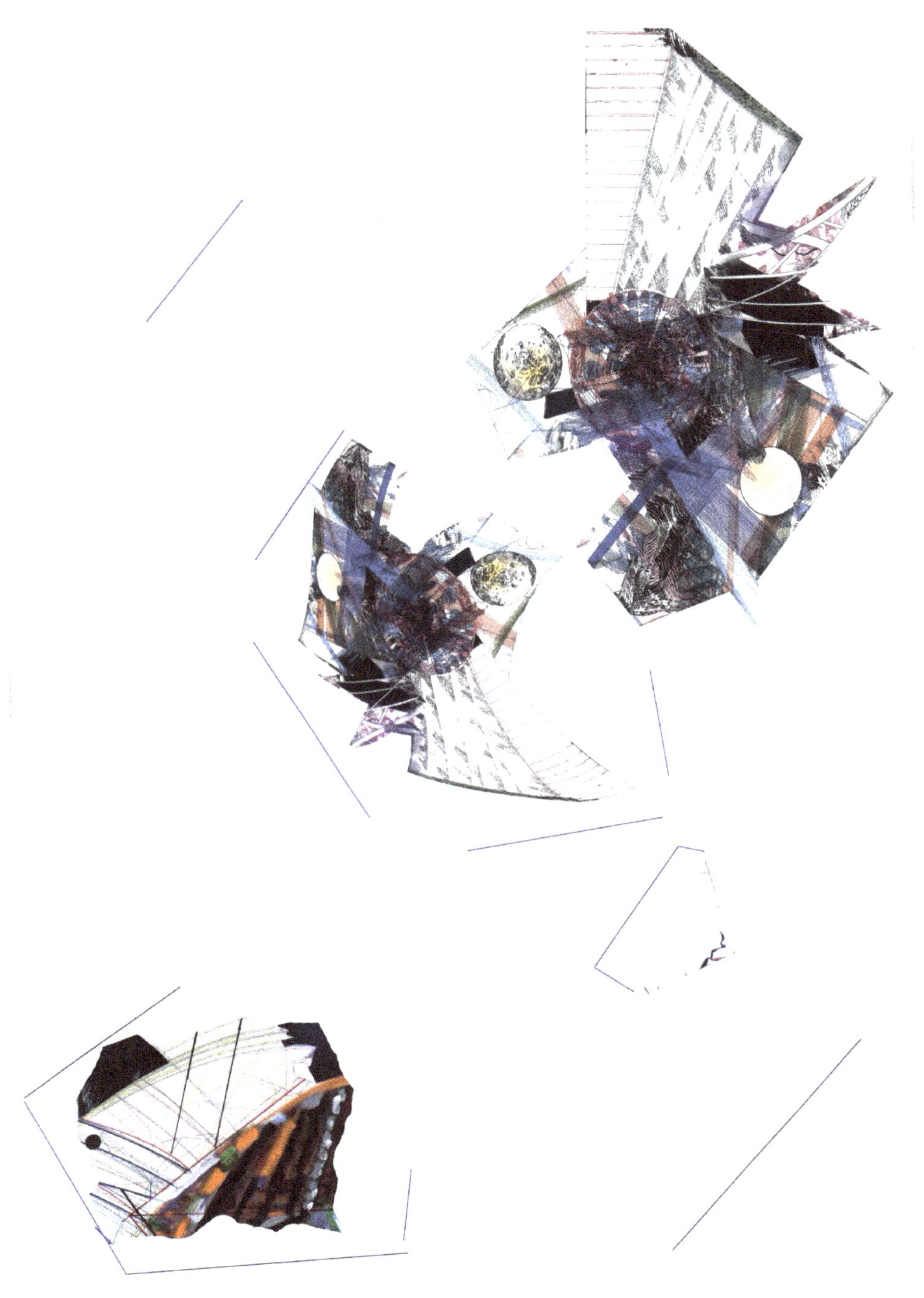

Tradition's Laughter
Mixed media on paper
44 x 30"
2019

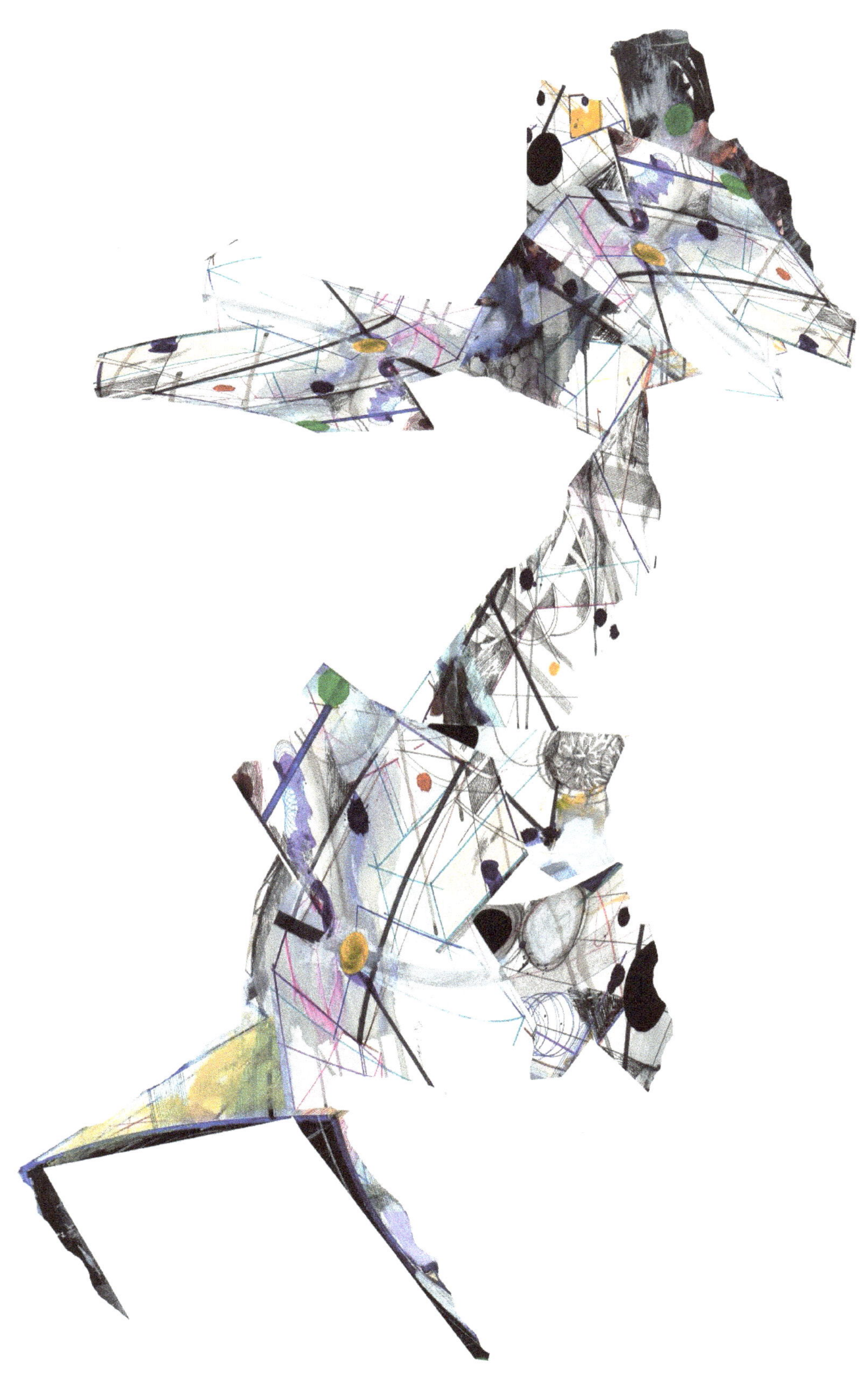

Particular System
Mixed media on paper
44 x 30"
2019

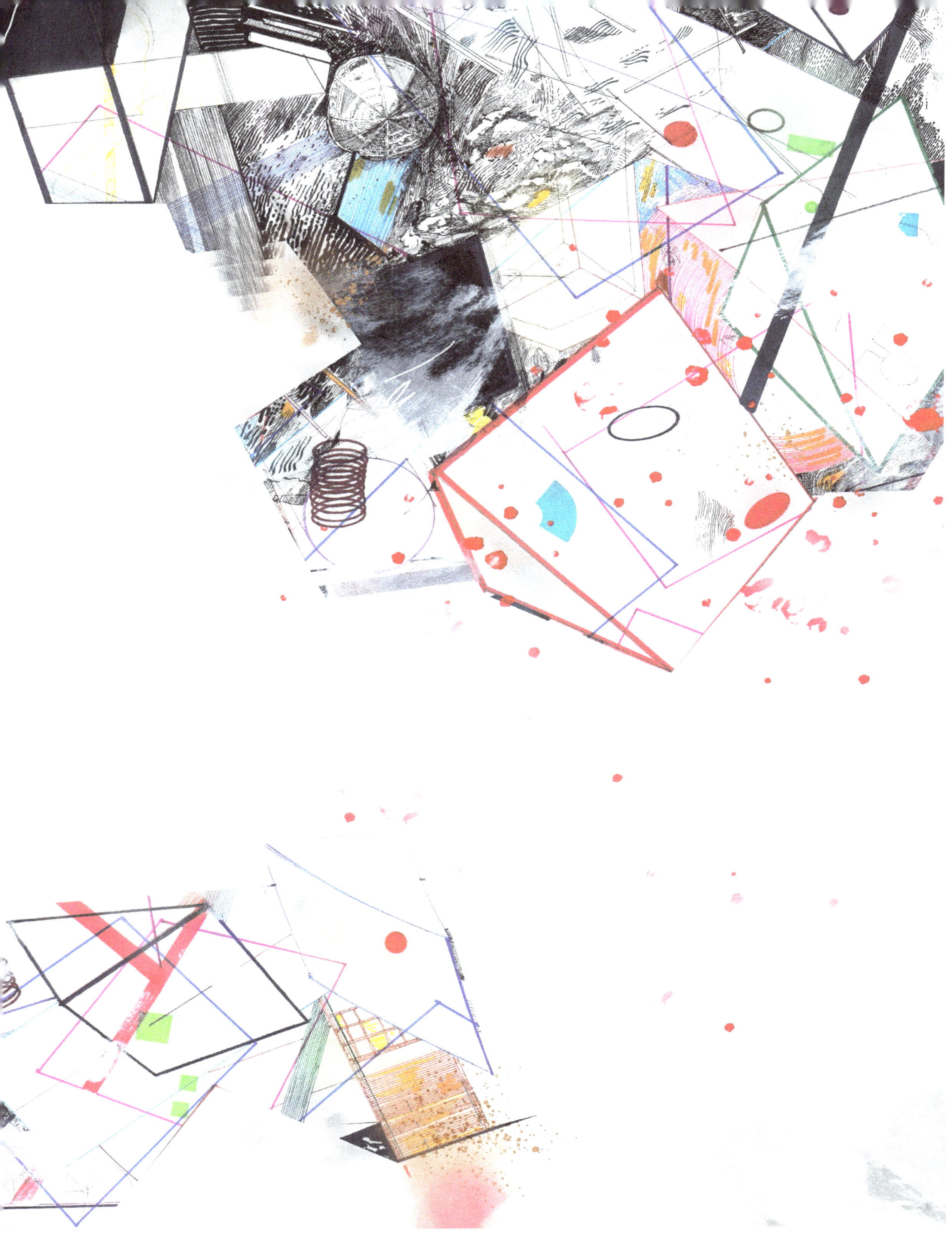

Harmony Series

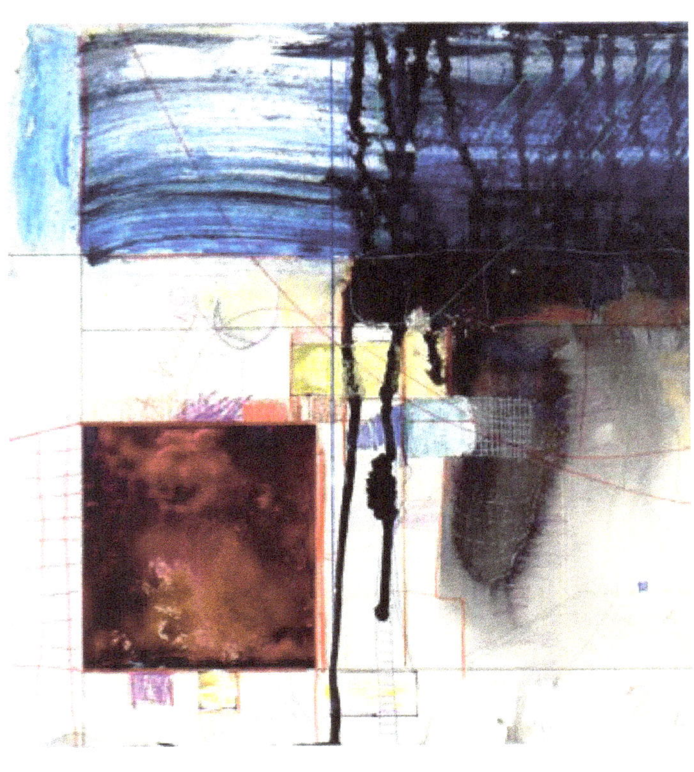

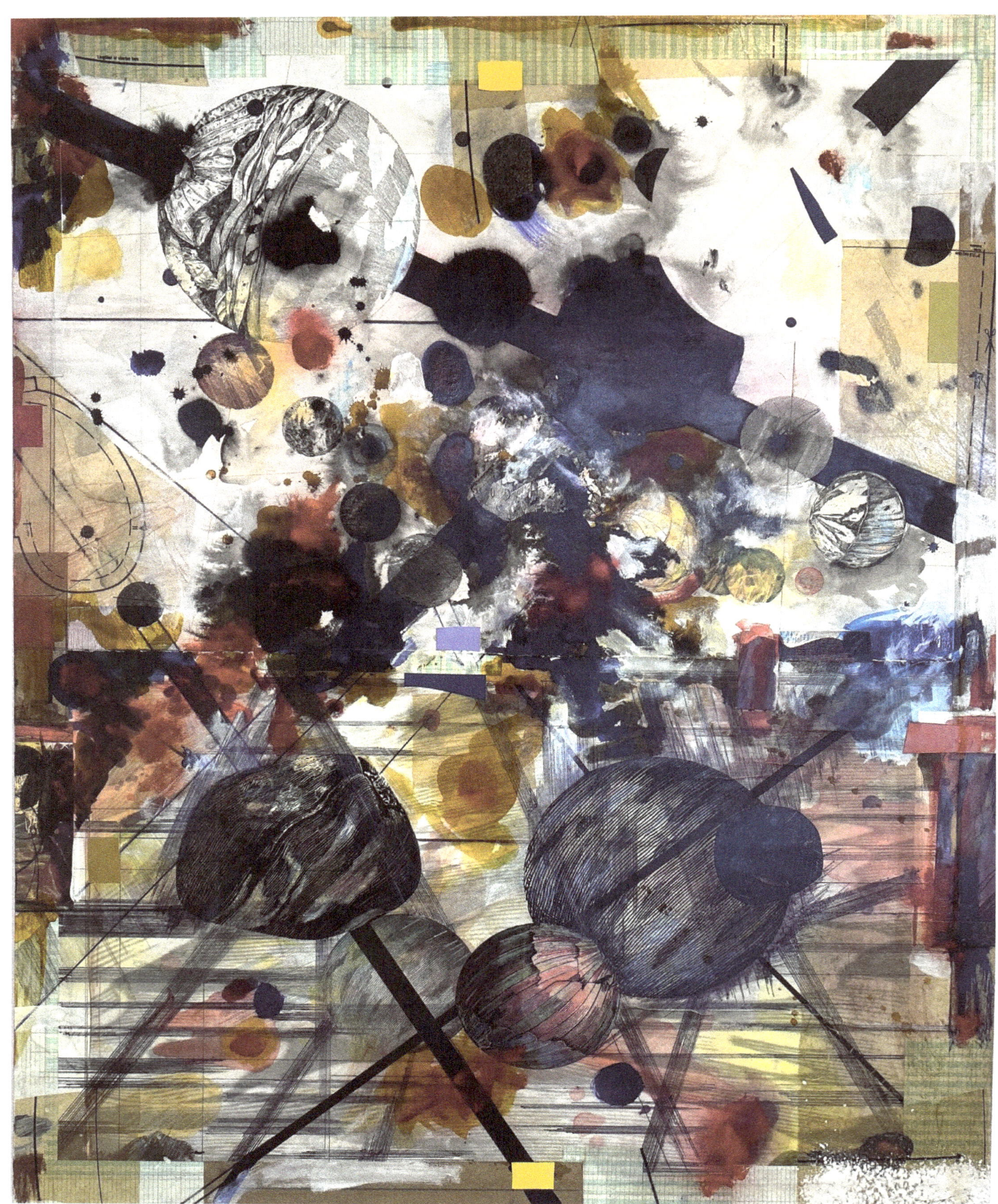

Harmony Large 1
Birch plywood, mono type digital print collage, paint
48 x 60"
2019

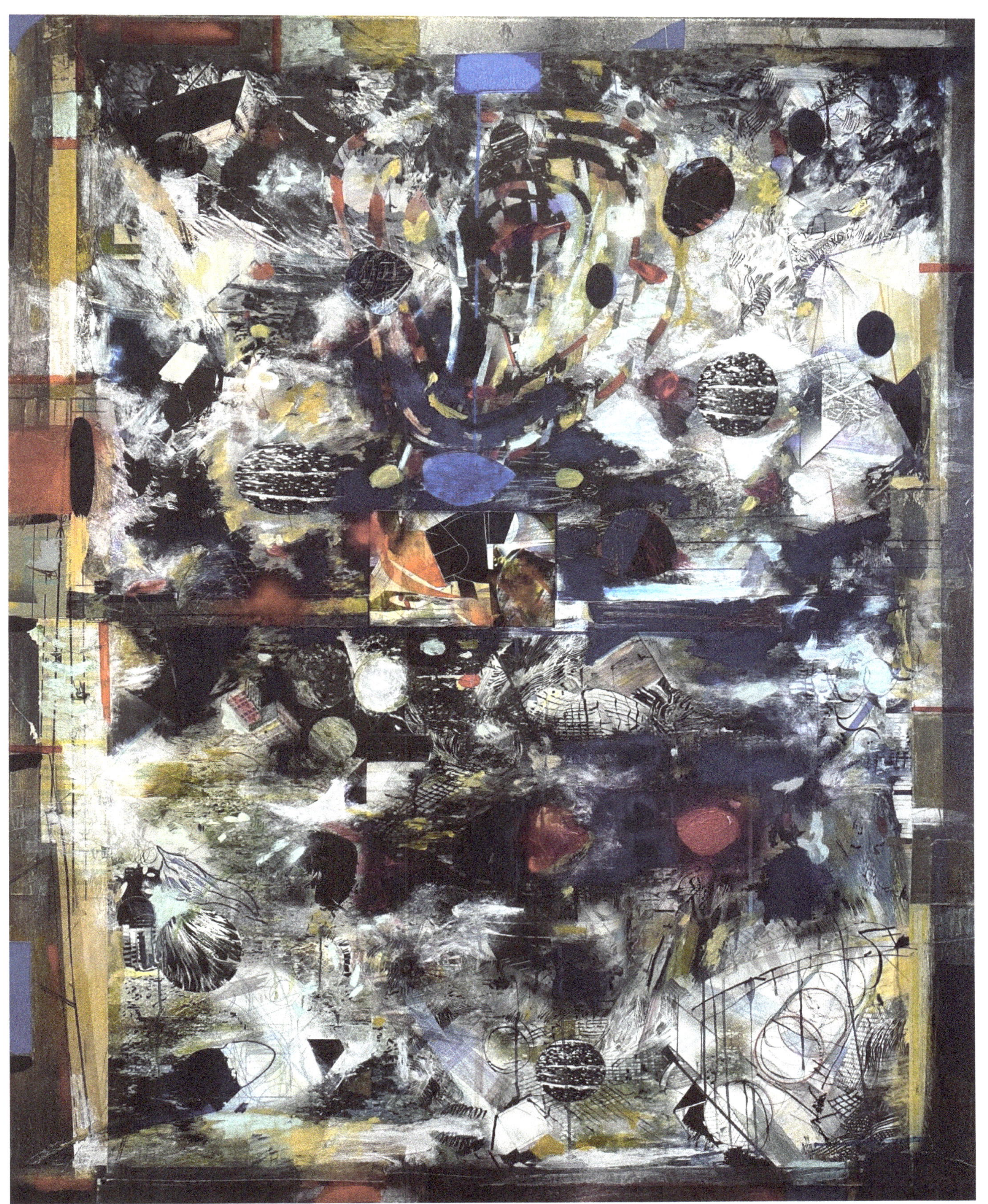

Harmony Large 2
Birch plywood, mono type digital print collage, paint
48 x 60"
2019

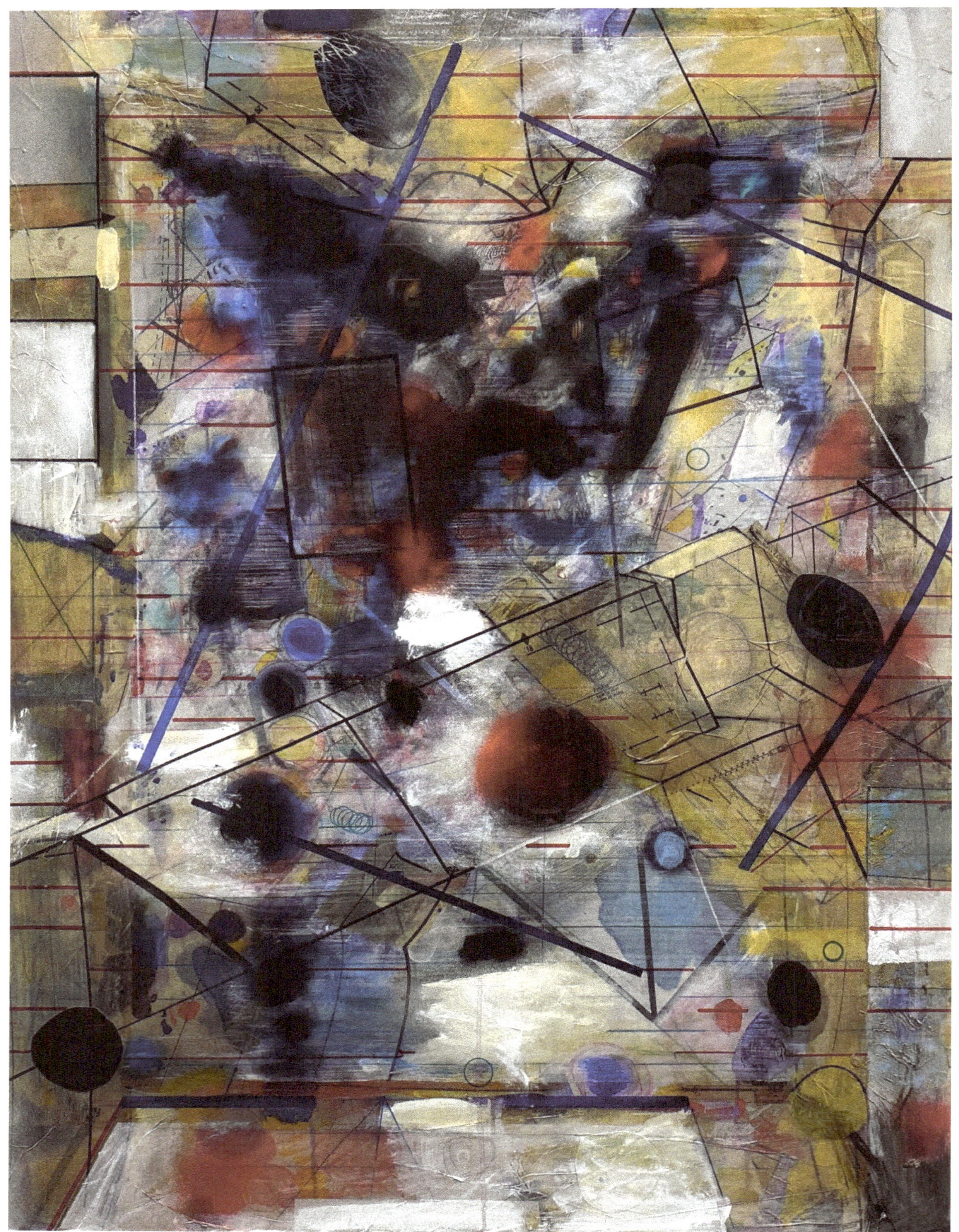

Harmony Designated
Birch plywood, mono type digital print
collage, paint
36 x 48"
2019

Comic Harmony →
Birch plywood, mono type digital print
collage, paint
36 x 48"
2019

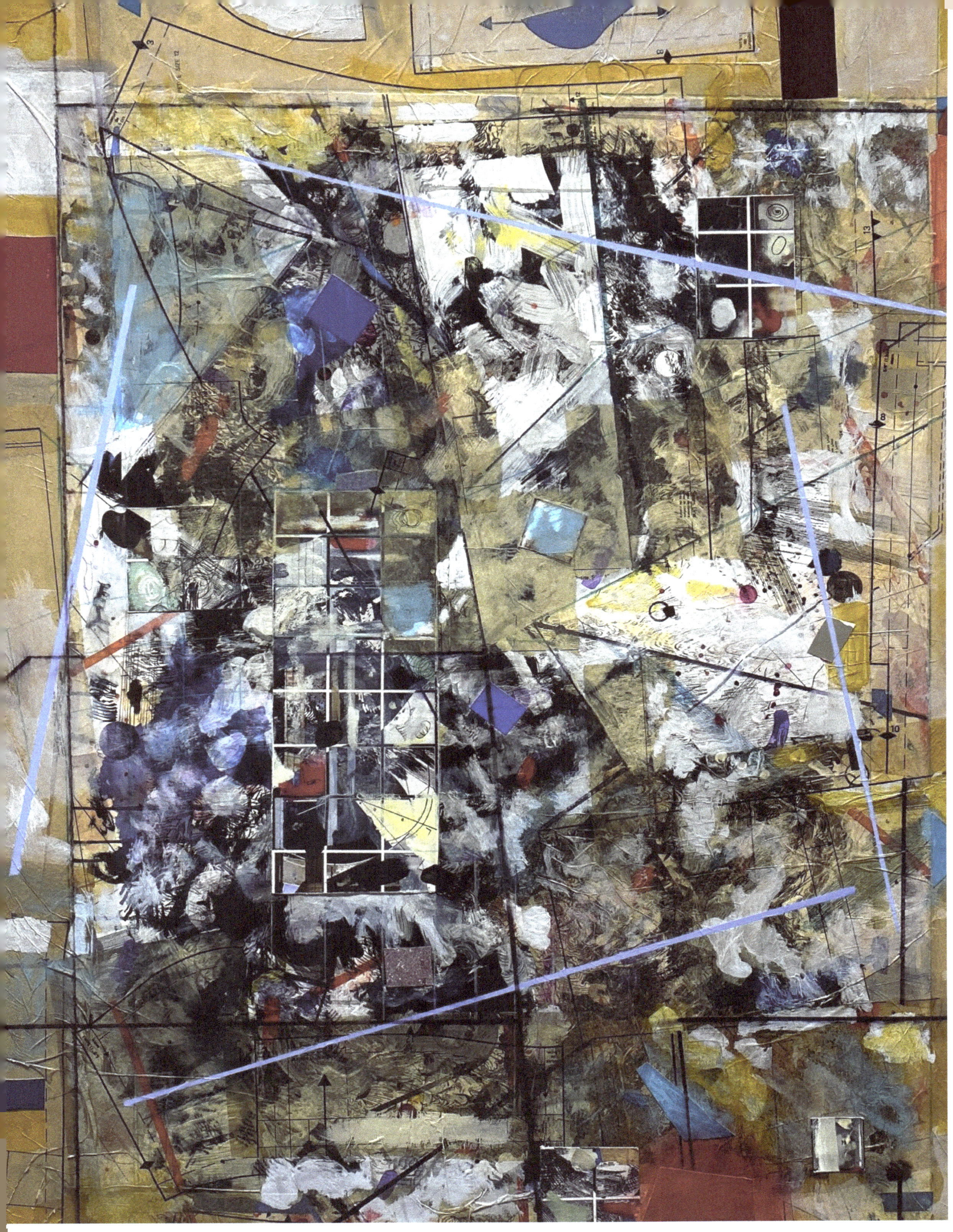

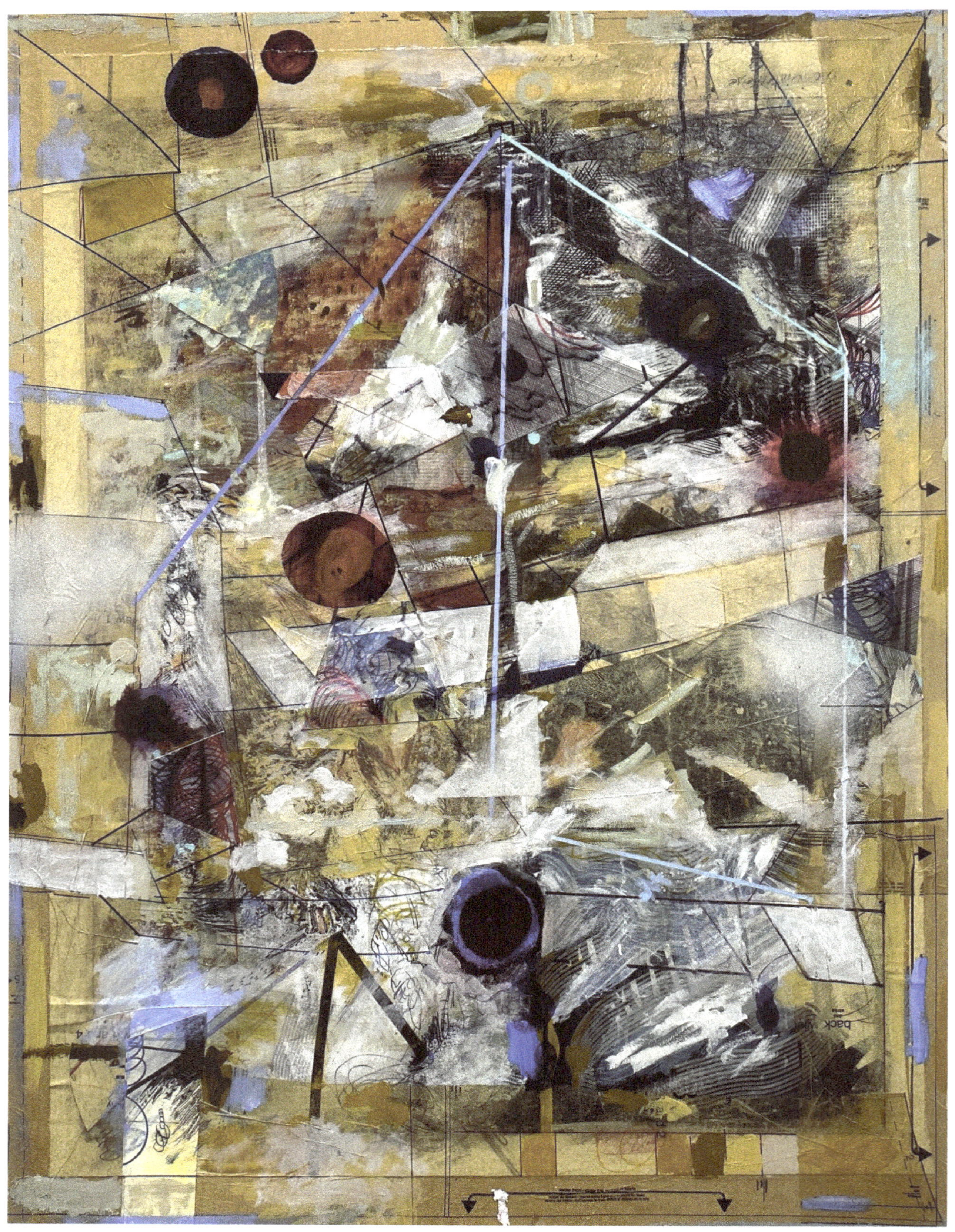

Harmony Demands
Birch plywood, mono type digital
print collage, paint
36 x 48"
2019

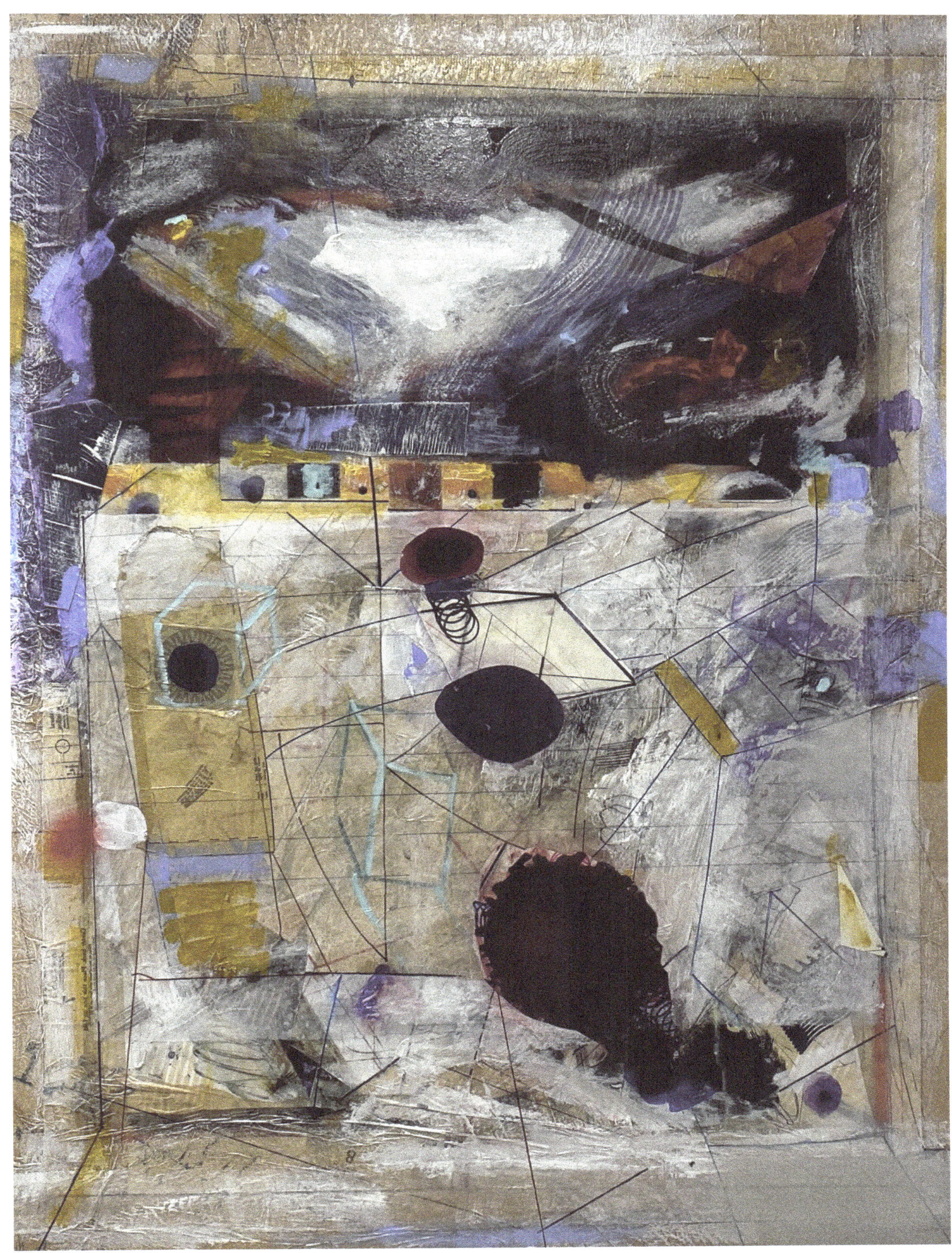

Harmony Bleached
Birch plywood, mono type digital
print collage, paint
36 x 48”
2019

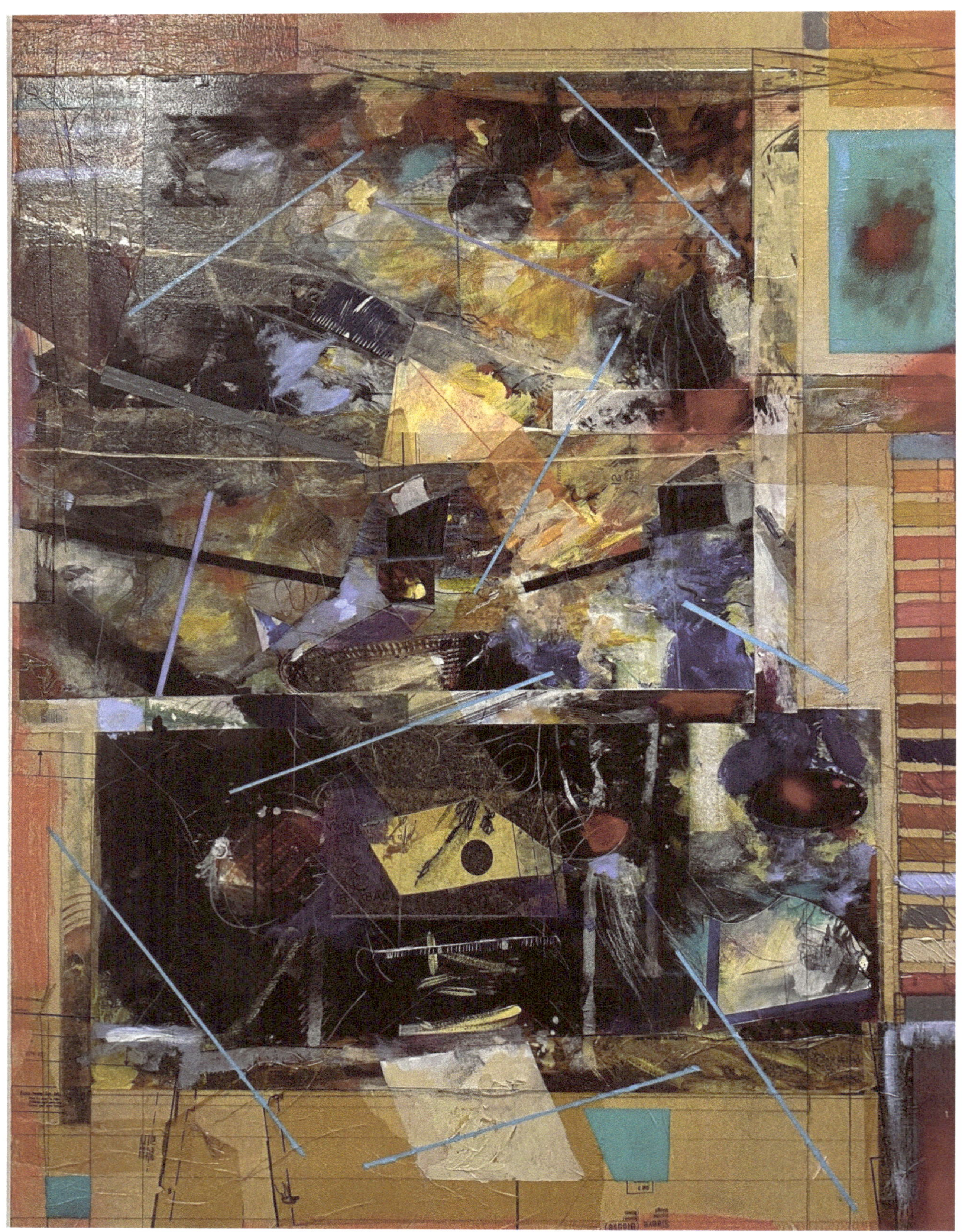

Harmony Separated
Birch plywood, mono type digital
print collage, paint
36 x 48"
2019

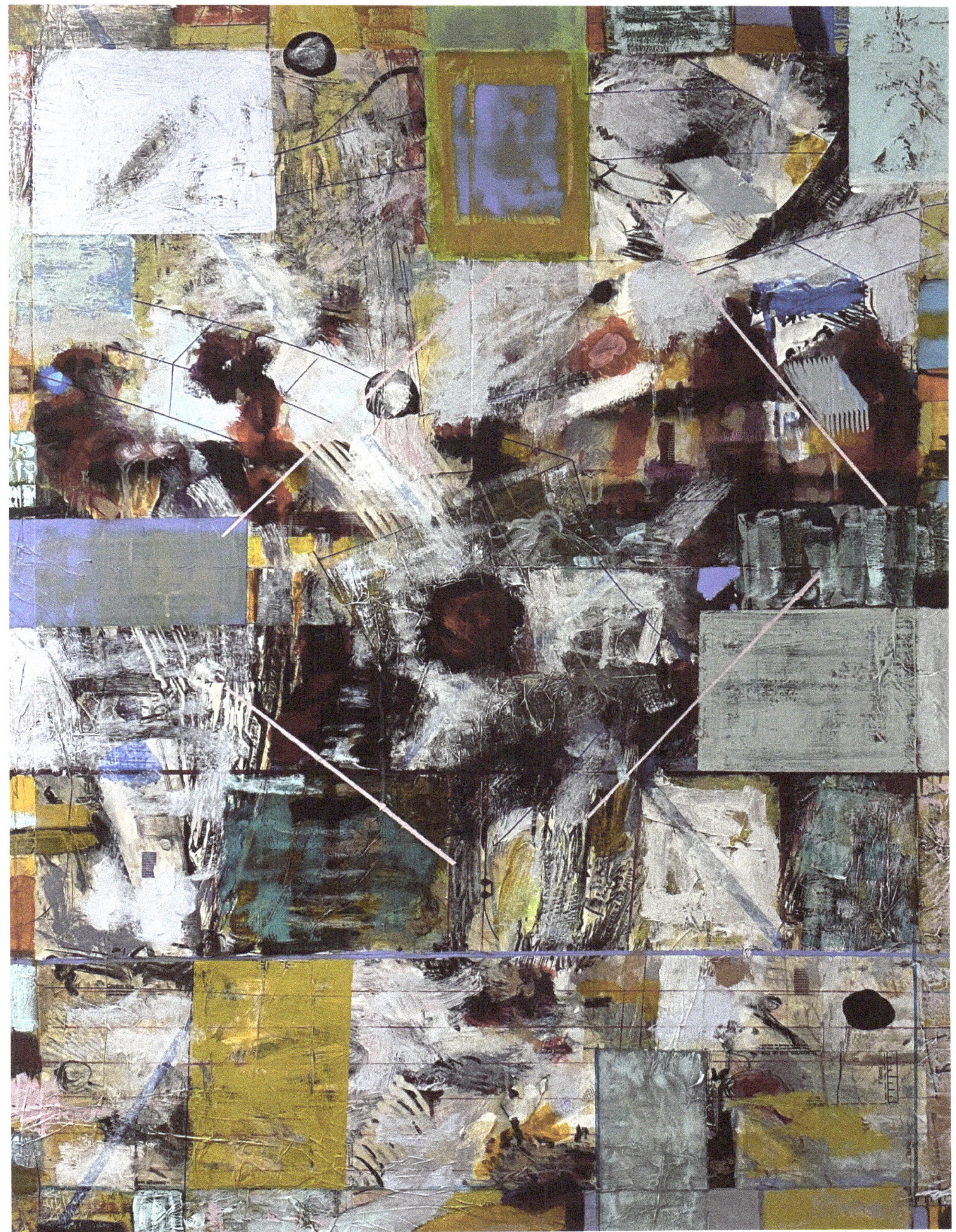

Observation
Birch plywood, mono type digital
print collage, paint
36 x 48"
2019

Phantom Series

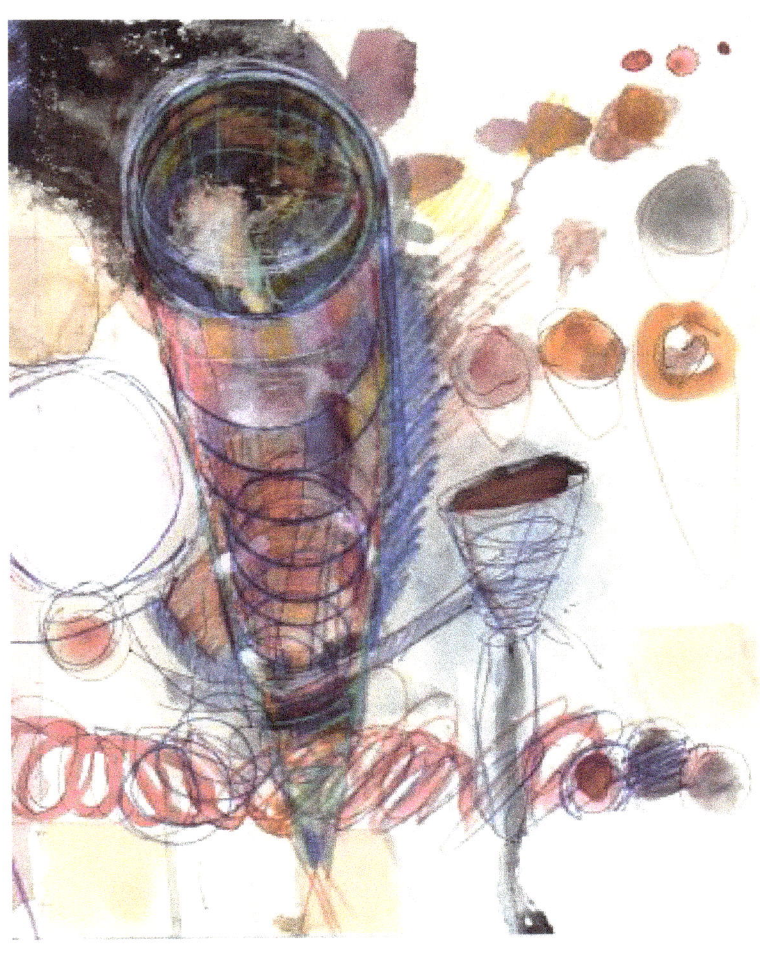

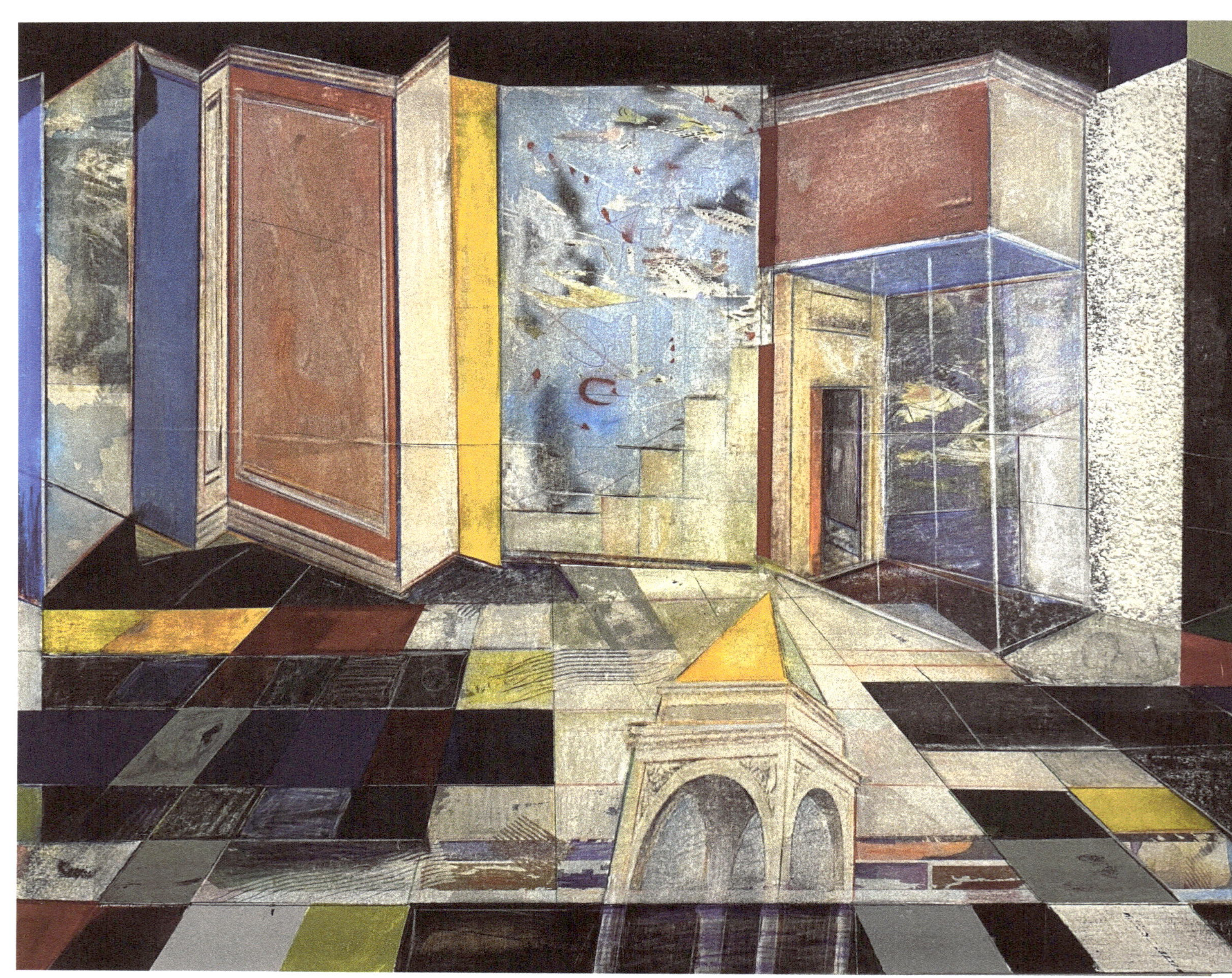

Phantom Stage 4
Birch plywood, mono type/ painting
30x24"
2019

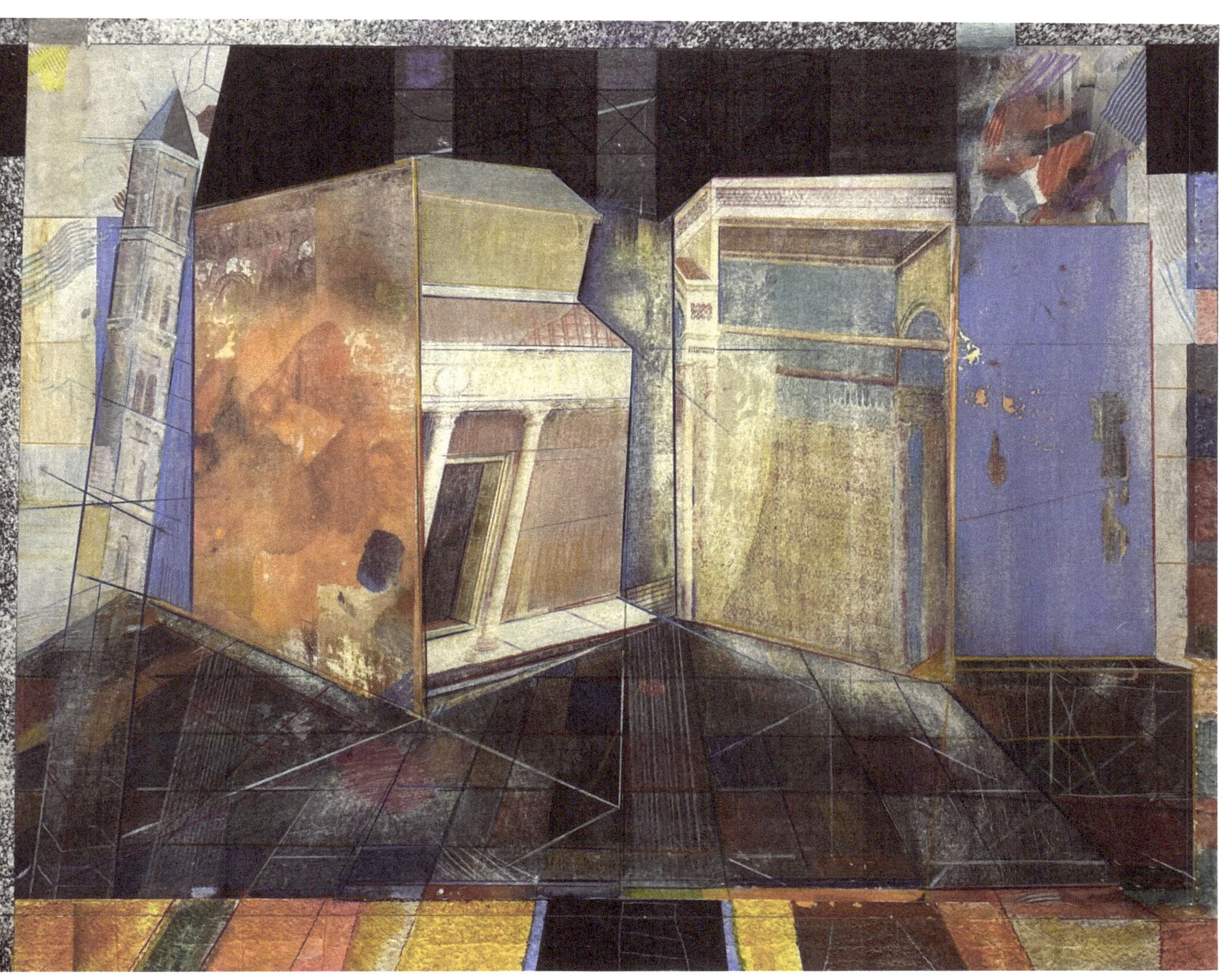

Phantom Stage 1
Birch plywood, mono type/ painting
30x24"
2019

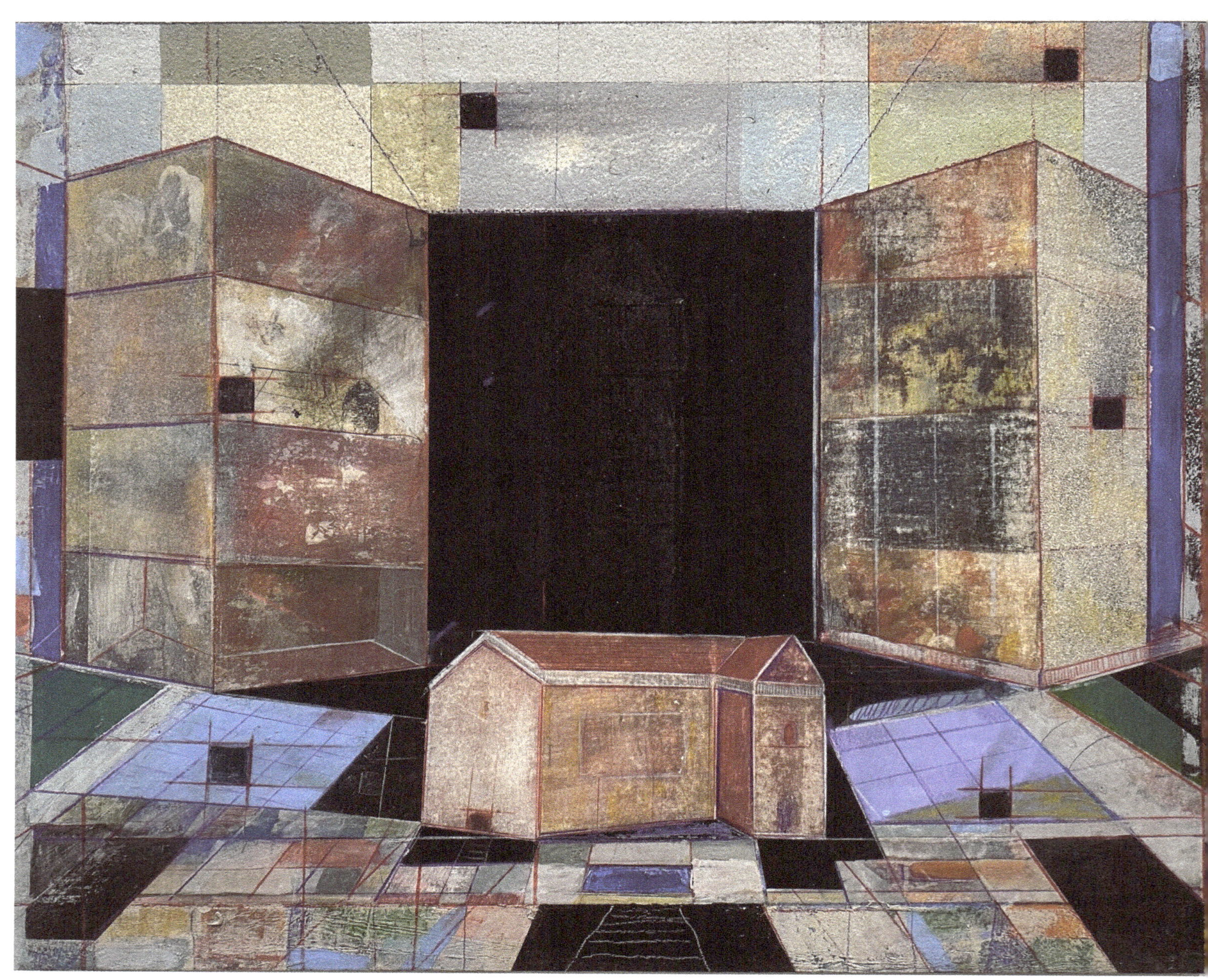

Phantom Stage 3
Birch plywood, digital pint monotype
digital print collage, paint
30x24"
2019

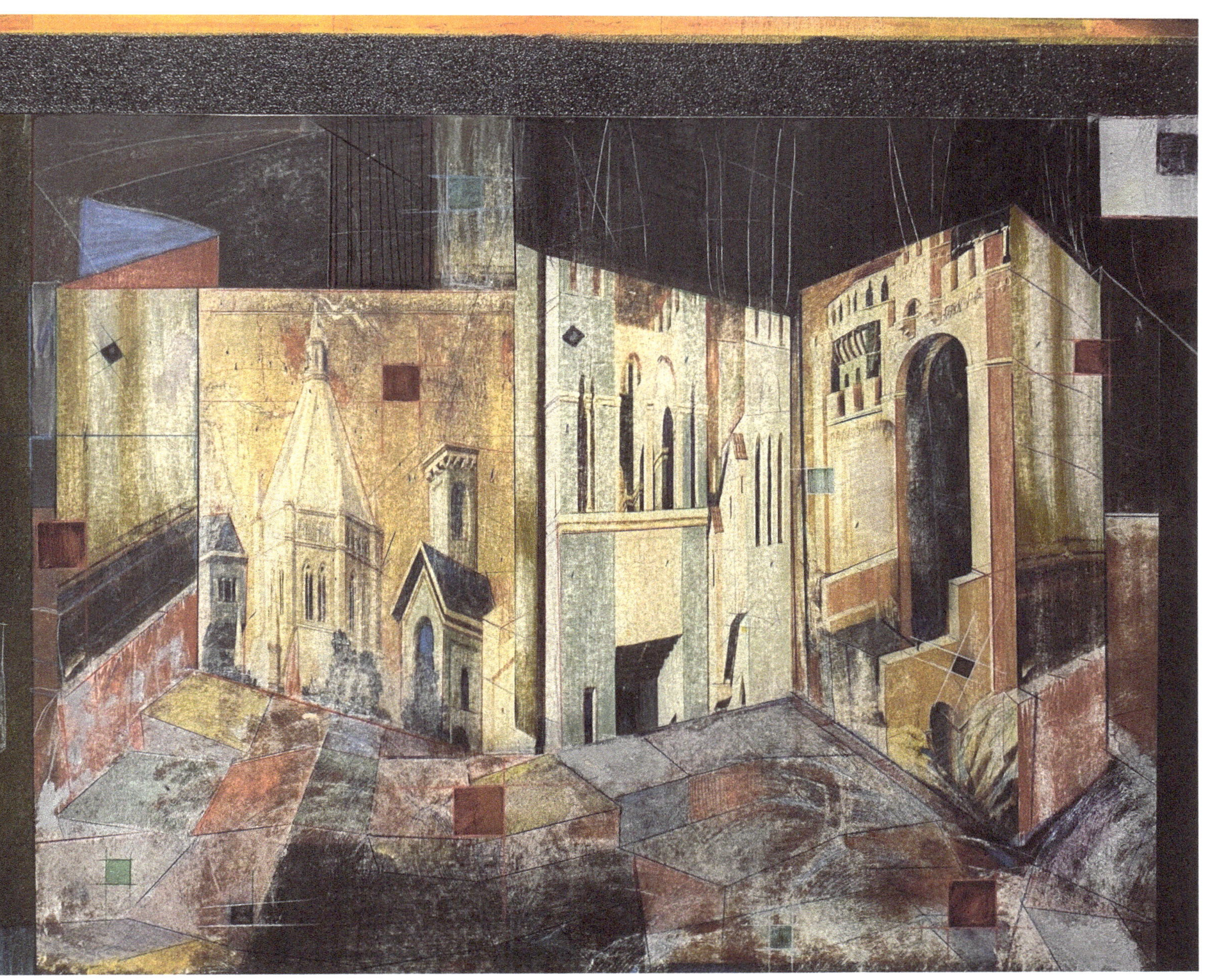

Phantom Stage 2
Birch plywood, digital pint monotype
digital print collage, paint
30x24"
2019

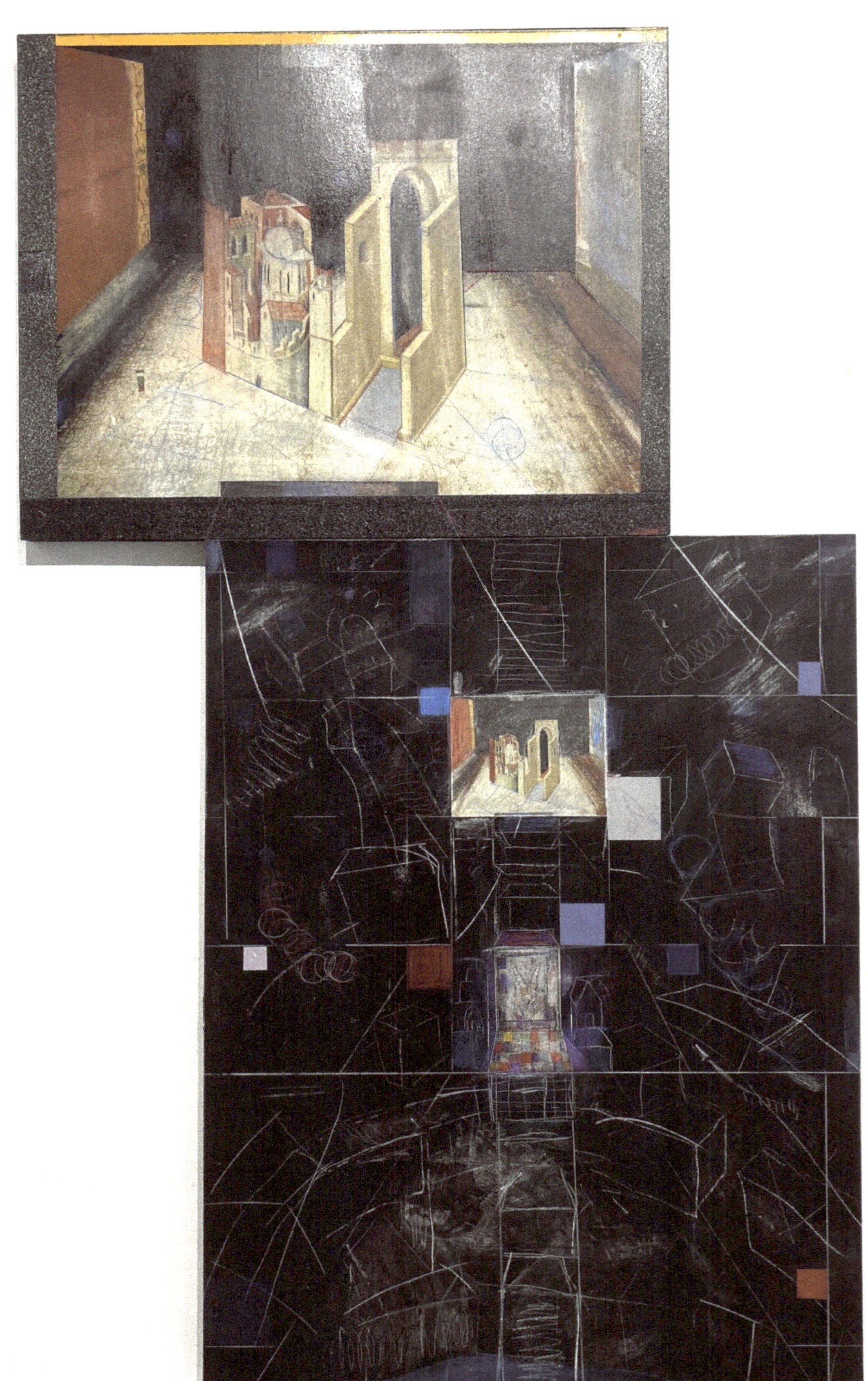

Phantom Stage 5
Birch plywood digital print monotype/painting
39 x 64"
2019

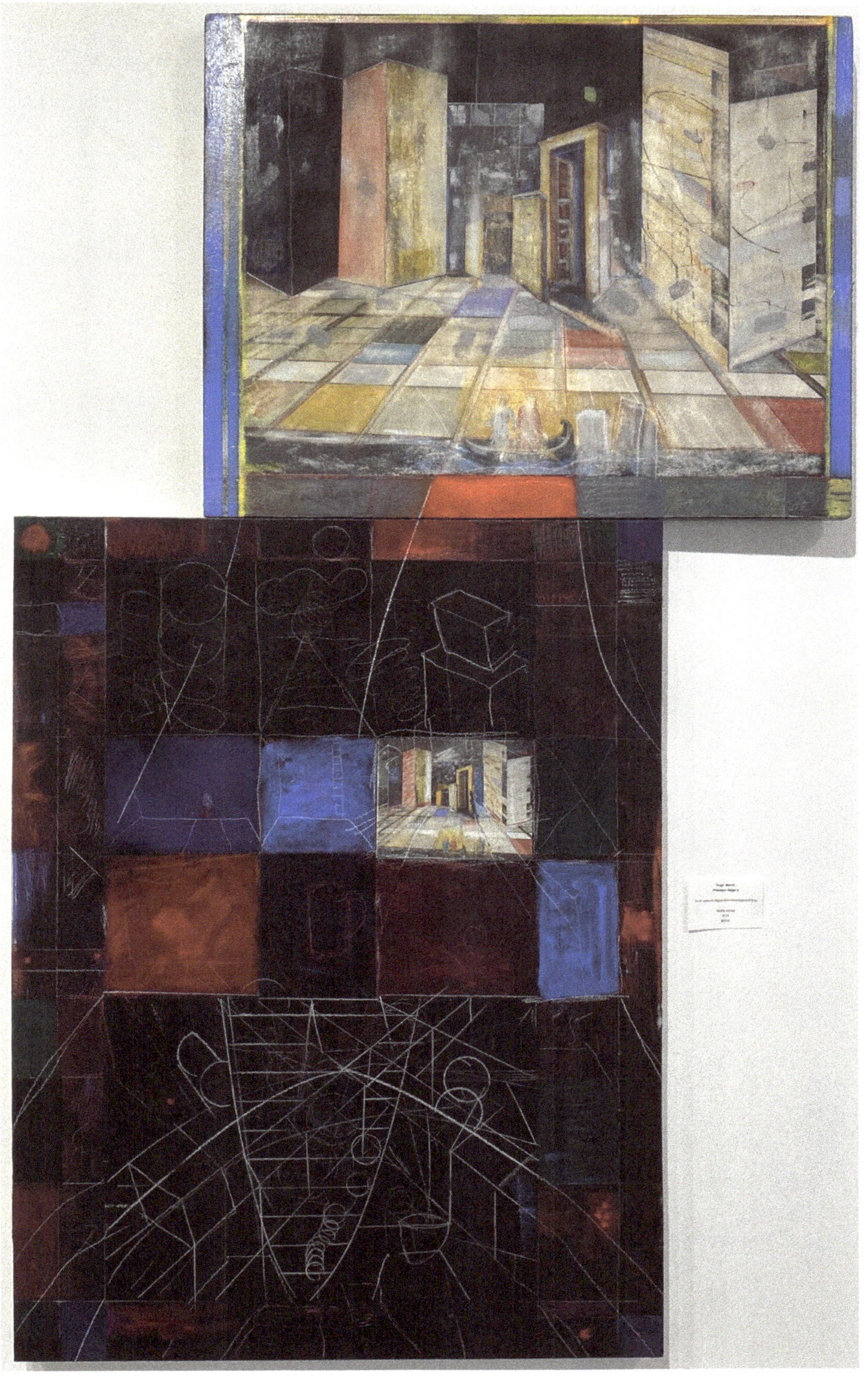

Phantom Stage 6
Birch plywood digital print monotype/painting
39 x 64"
2019

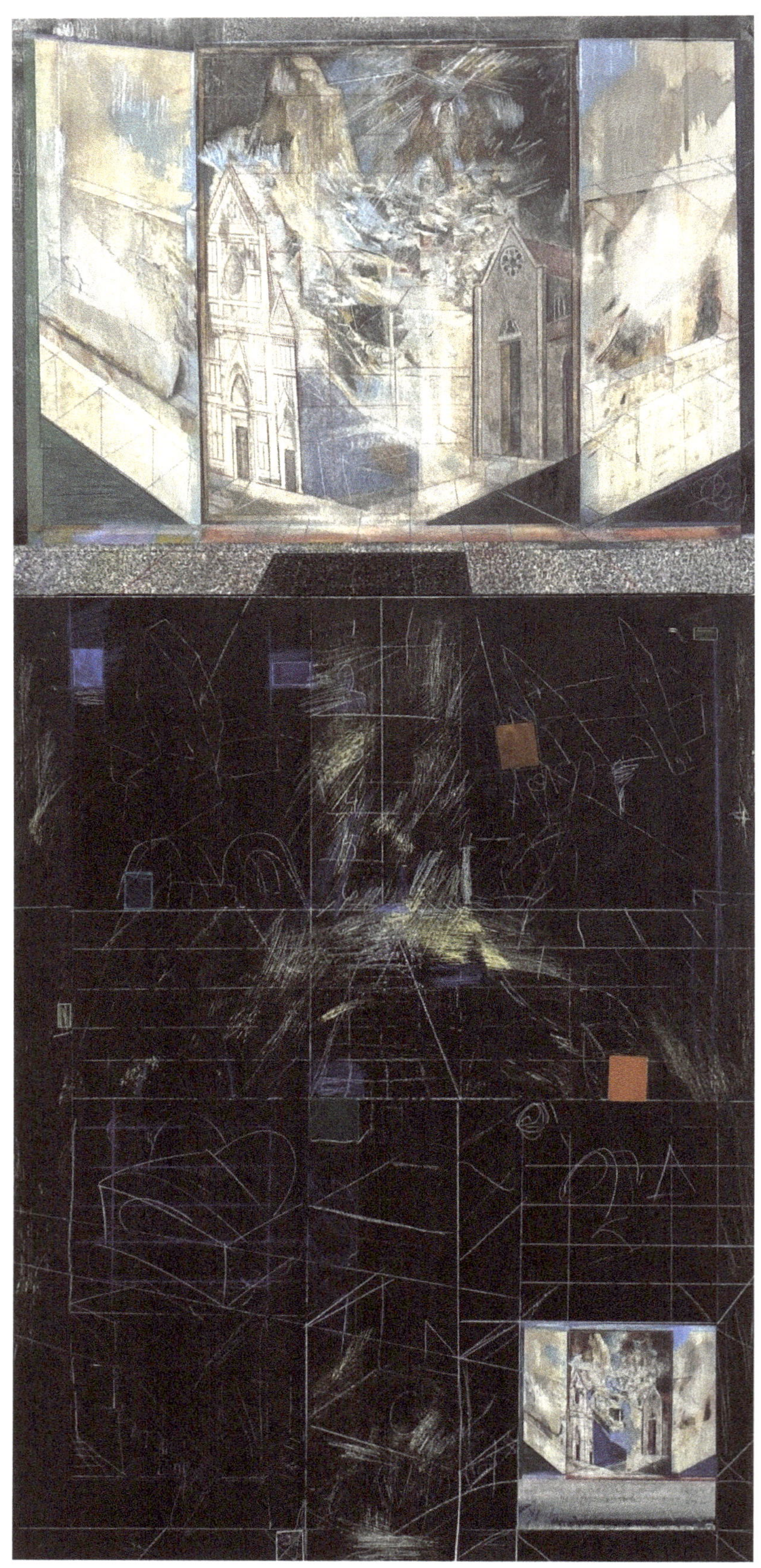

Phantom Stage 5
Birch plywood digital print monotype/painting
39 x 64"
2019

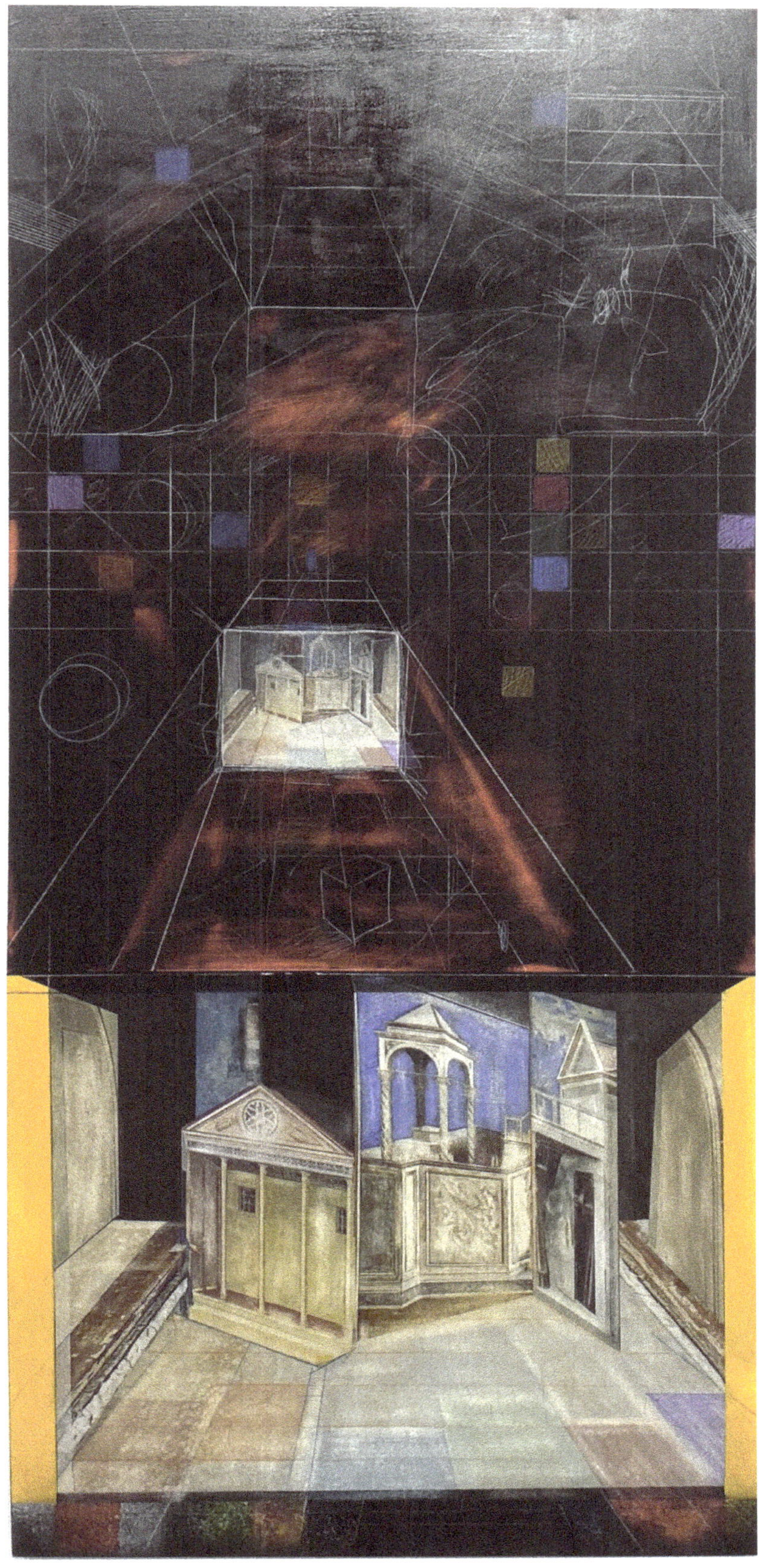

Phantom Stage 6
Birch plywood digital print monotype/painting
39 x 64"
2019

Vital Junction Series

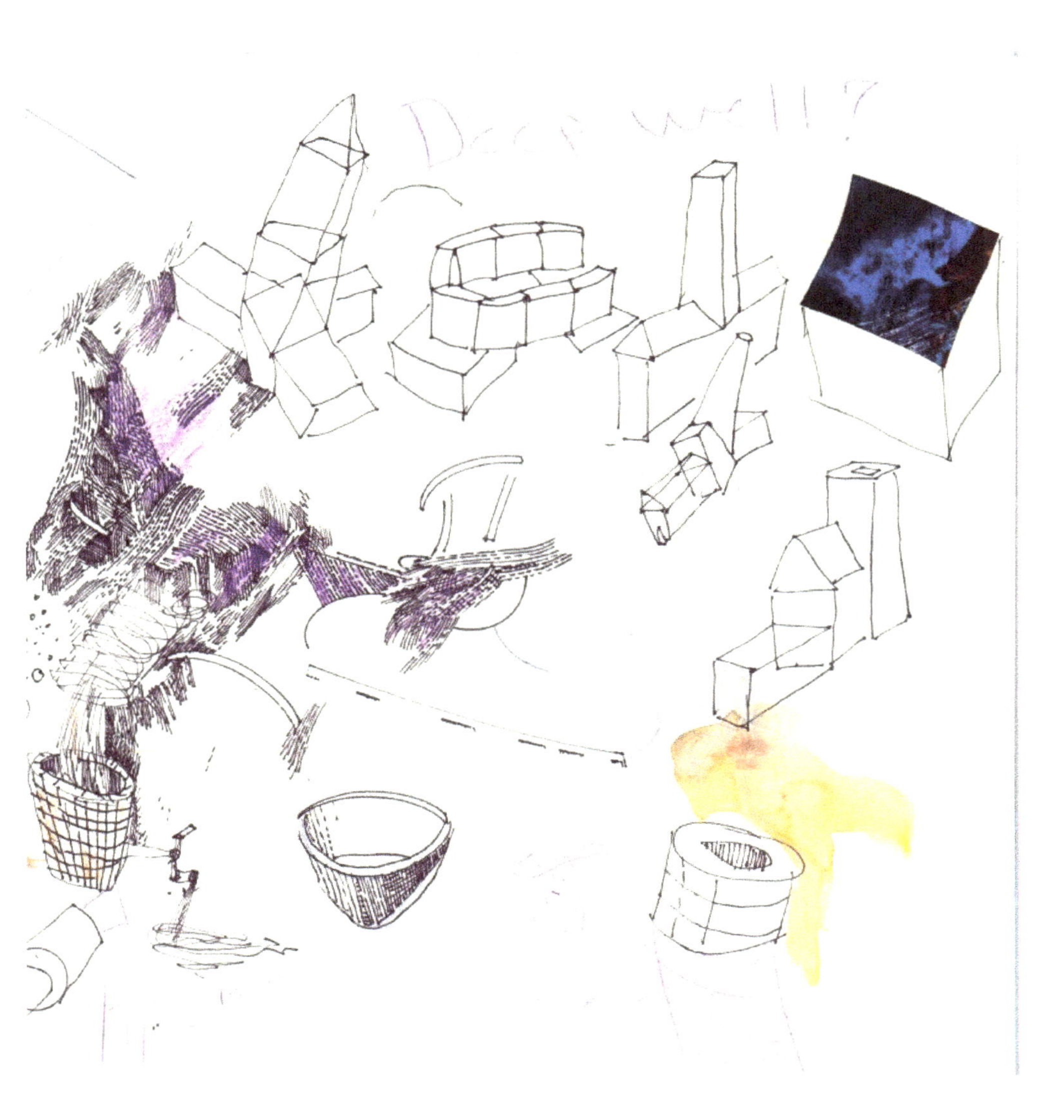

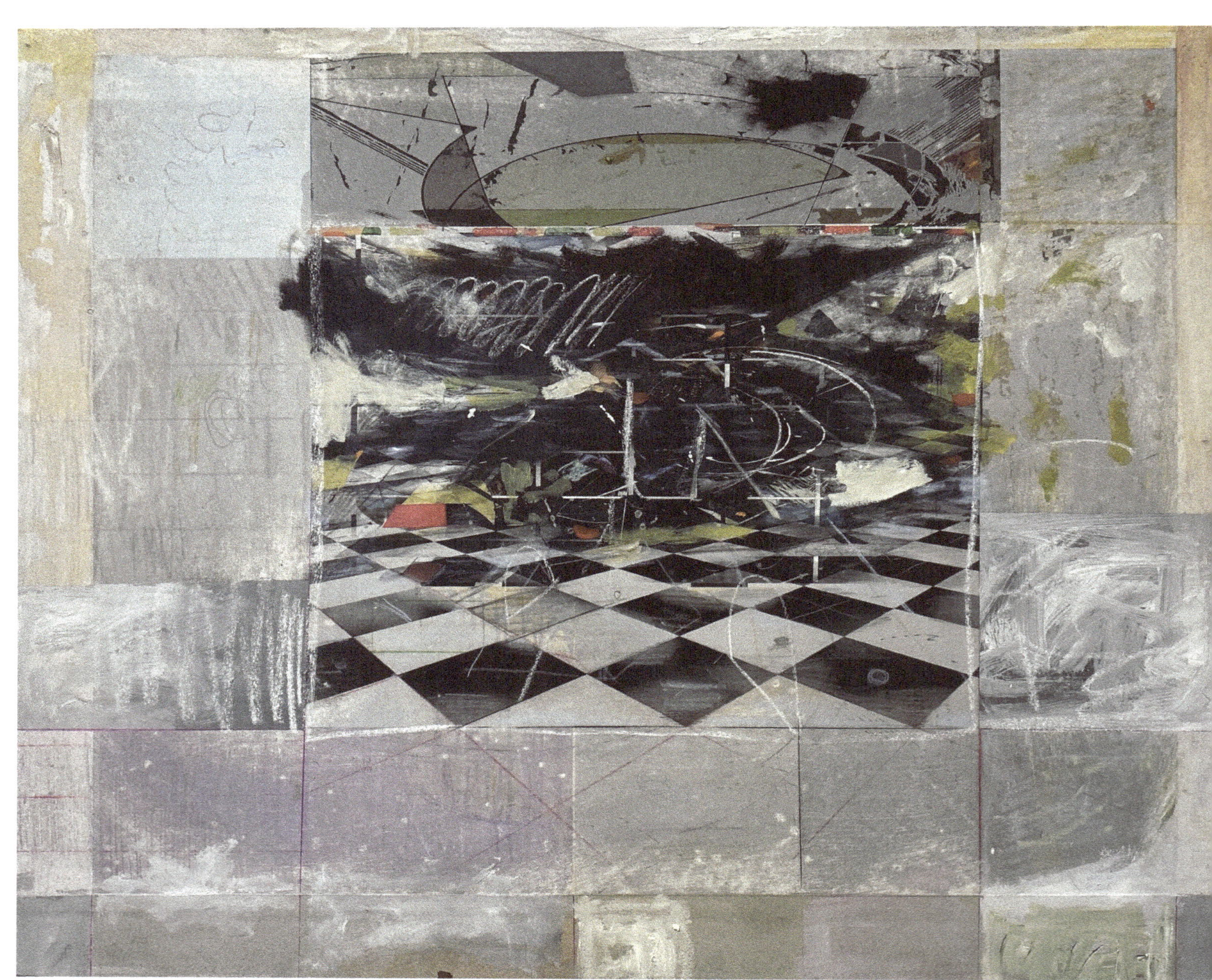

Renewing Joy 1
Birch plywood, mono type digital
collage, paint
30x24"
2019

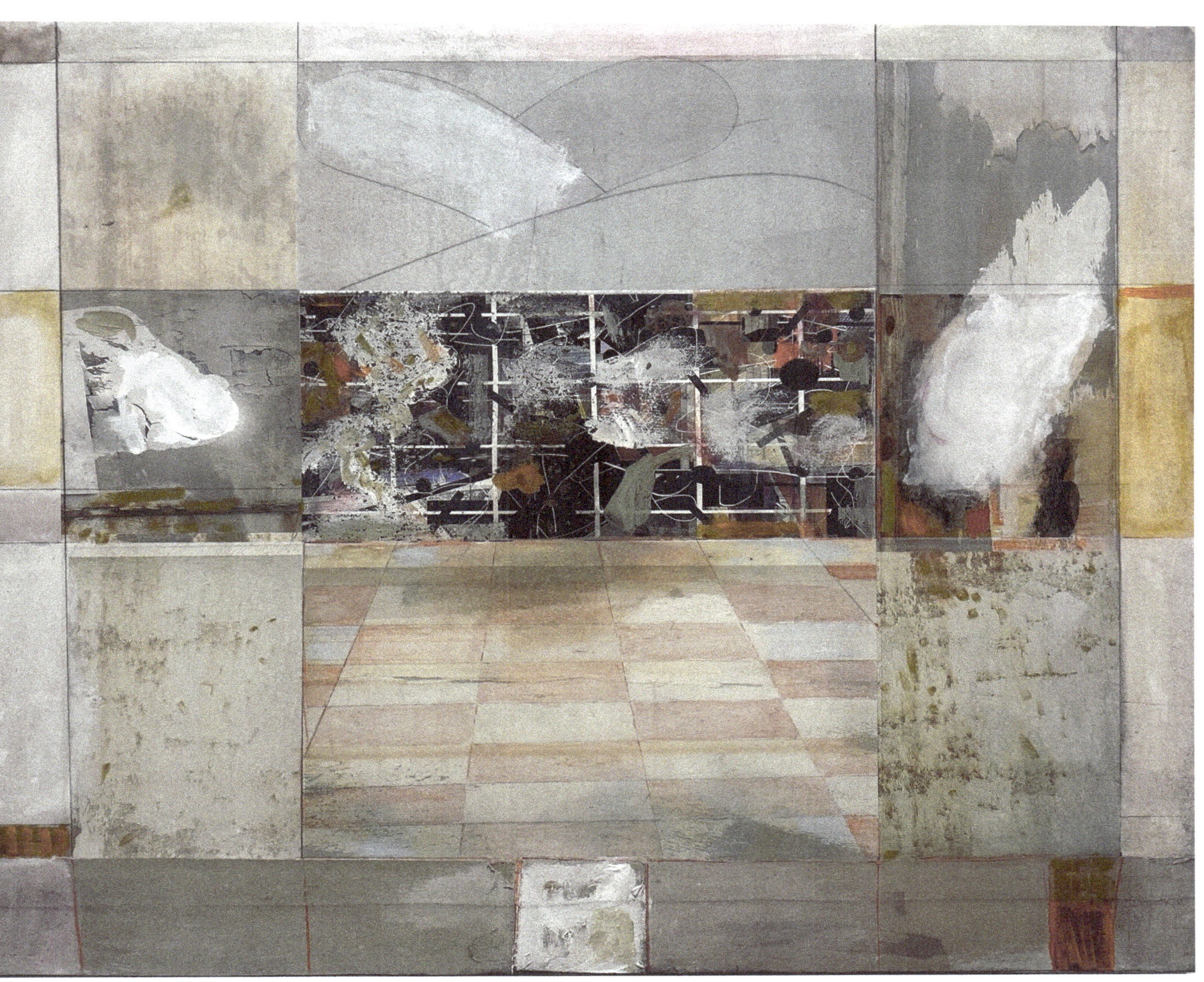

Renewing Joy 2
Birch plywood, mono type digital
collage, paint
30x24"
2019

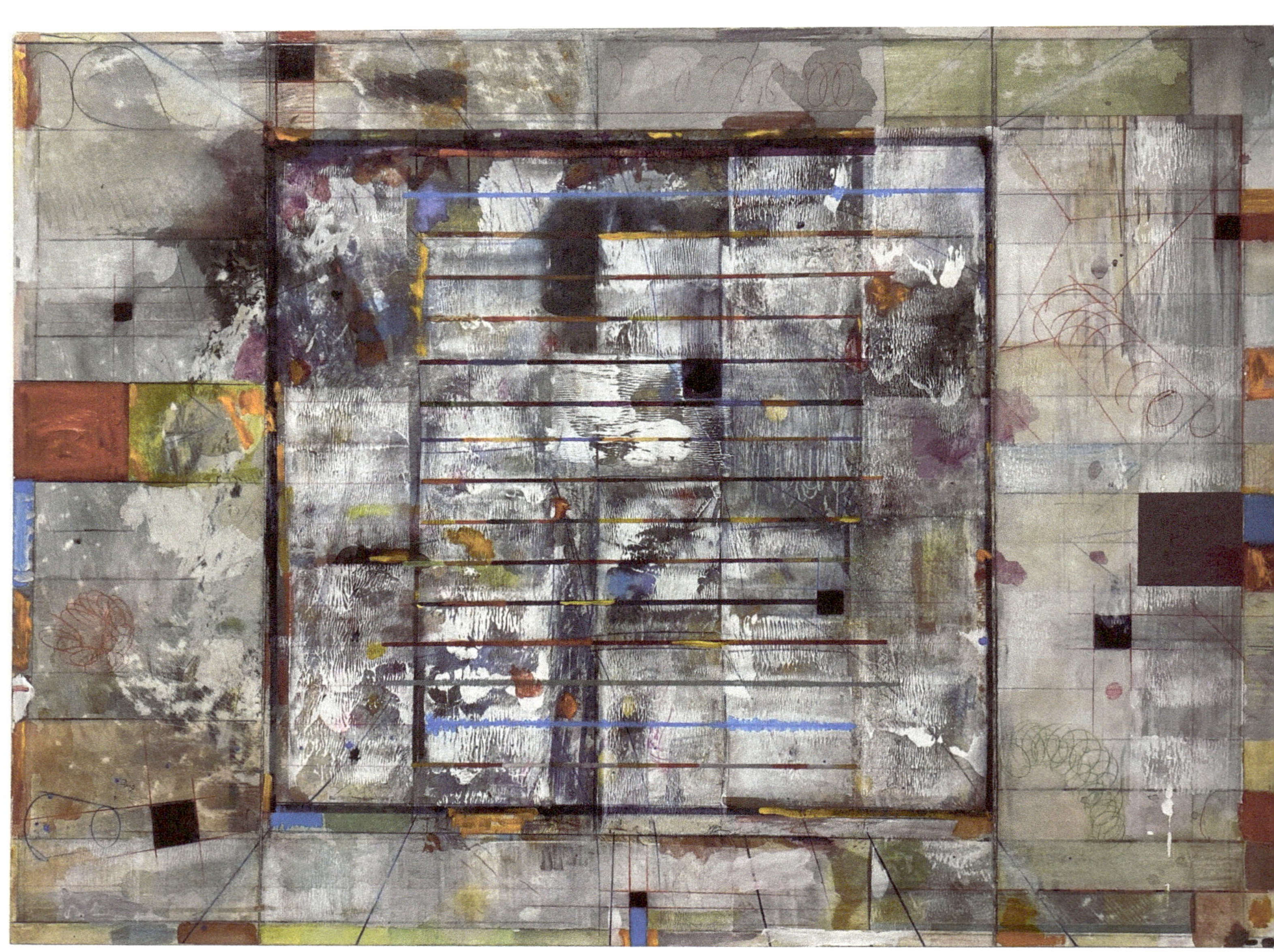

Vital Junction 1
Birch plywood, mono type digital
collage, paint
40x30"
2019

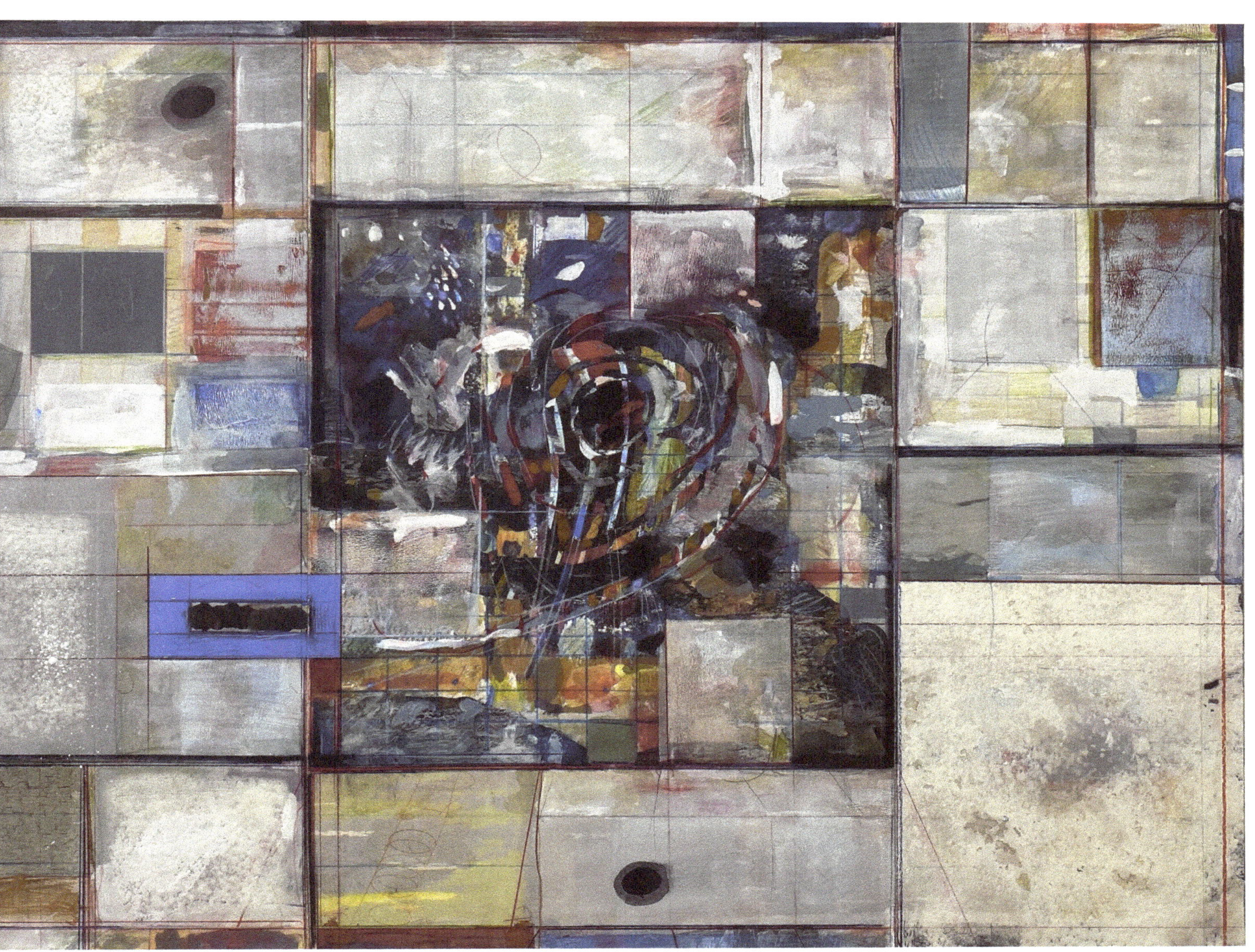

Vital Junction 2
Birch plywood, mono type digital
collage, paint
40x30"
2019

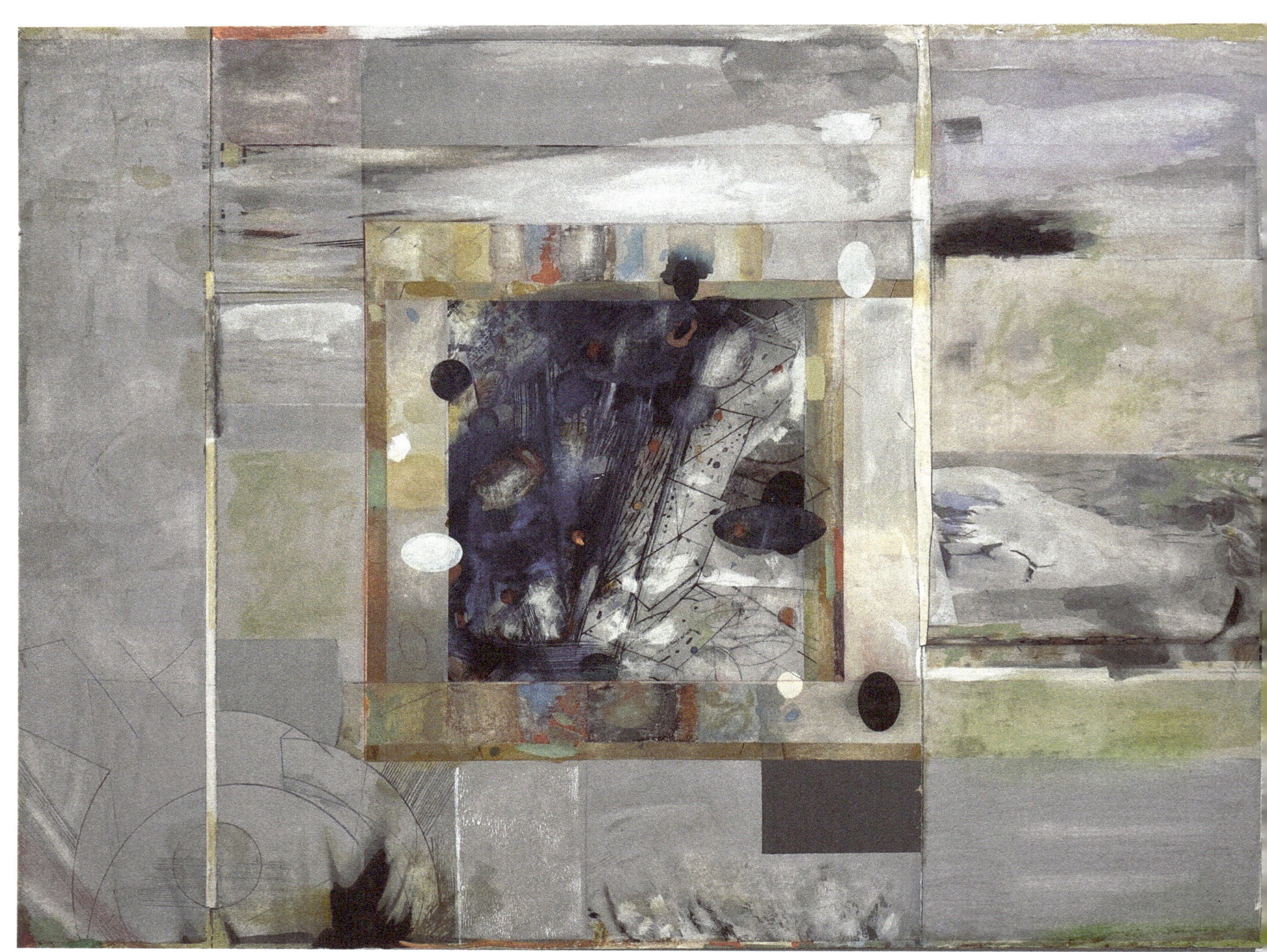

Vital Junction 3
Birch plywood, mono type digital
collage, paint
40x30"
2019

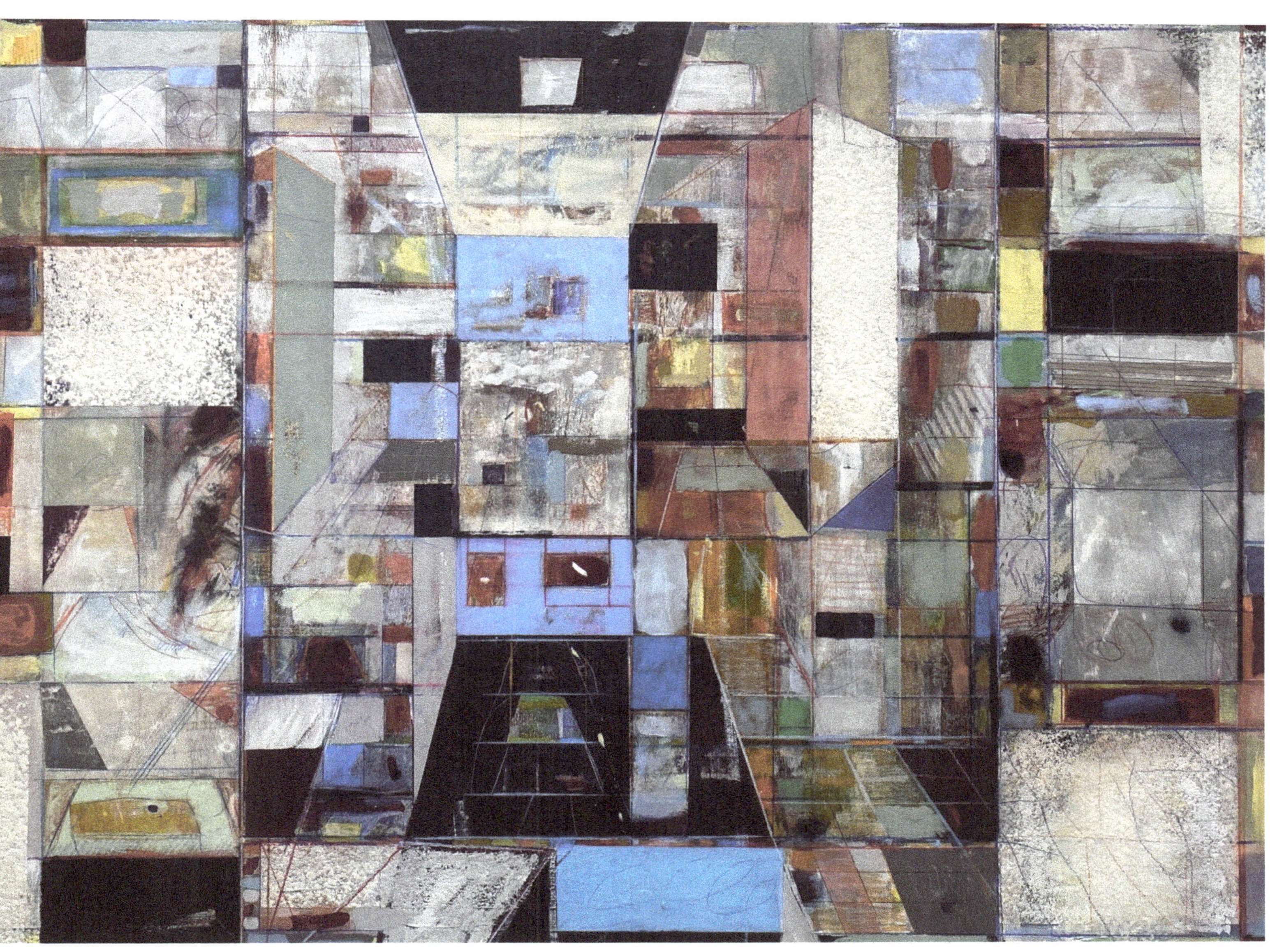

Vital Junction 4
Birch plywood, mono type digital
collage, paint
40x30"
2019

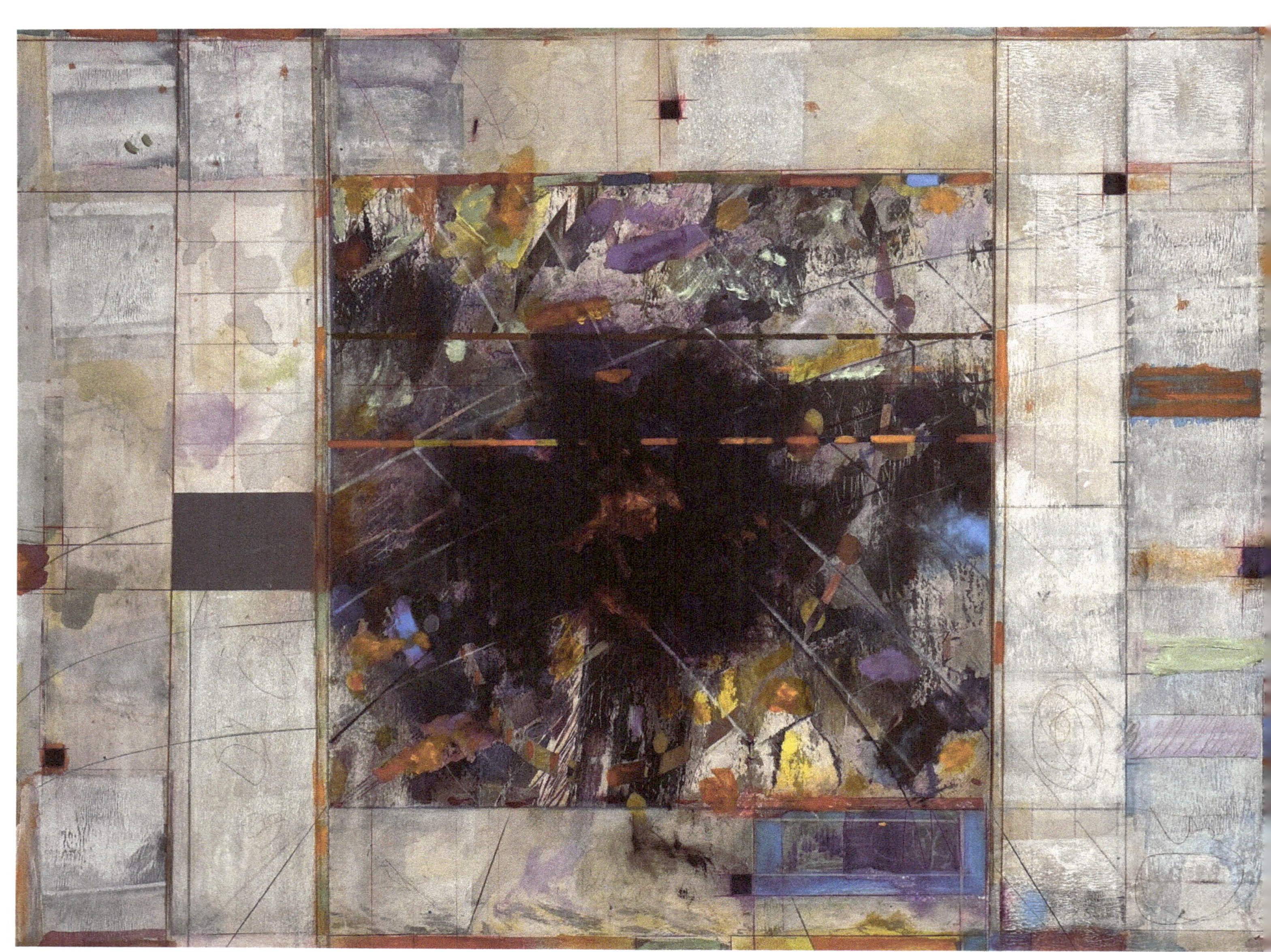

Vital Junction 5
Birch plywood, mono type digital
collage, paint
40x30"
2019

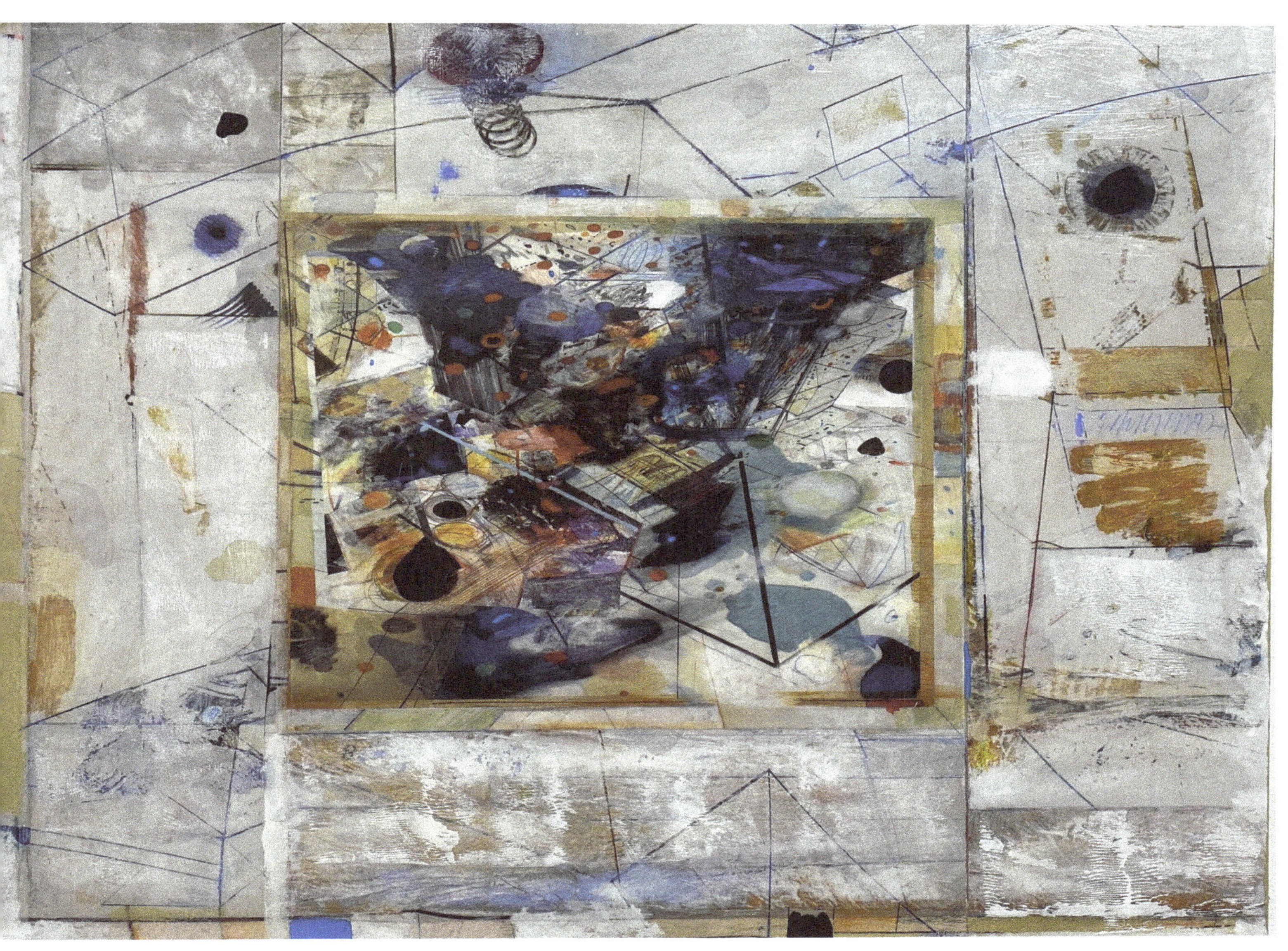

Vital Junction 6
Birch plywood, mono type digital
collage, paint
40x30"
2019

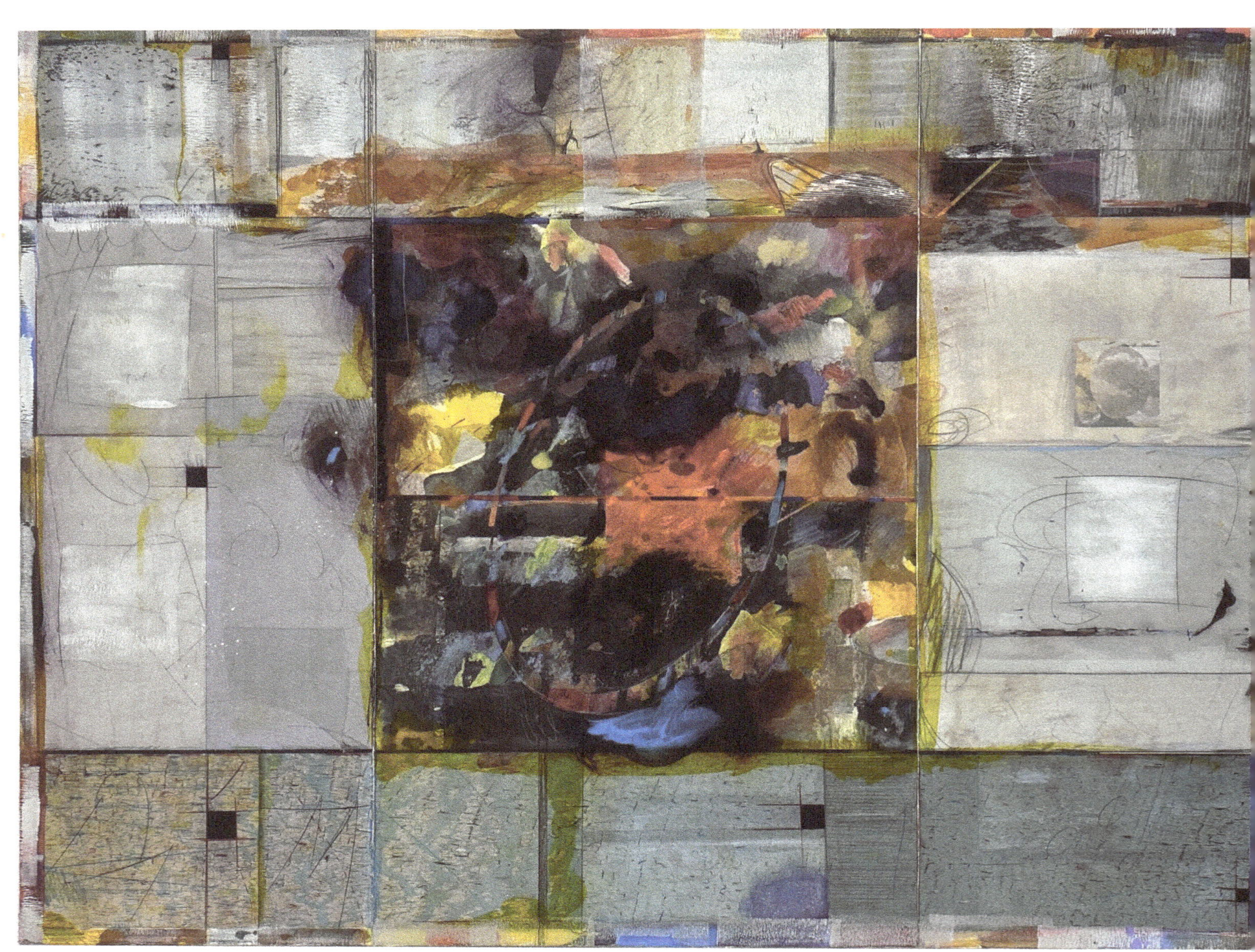

Vital Junction 5
Birch plywood, mono type digital
collage, paint
40x30"
2019

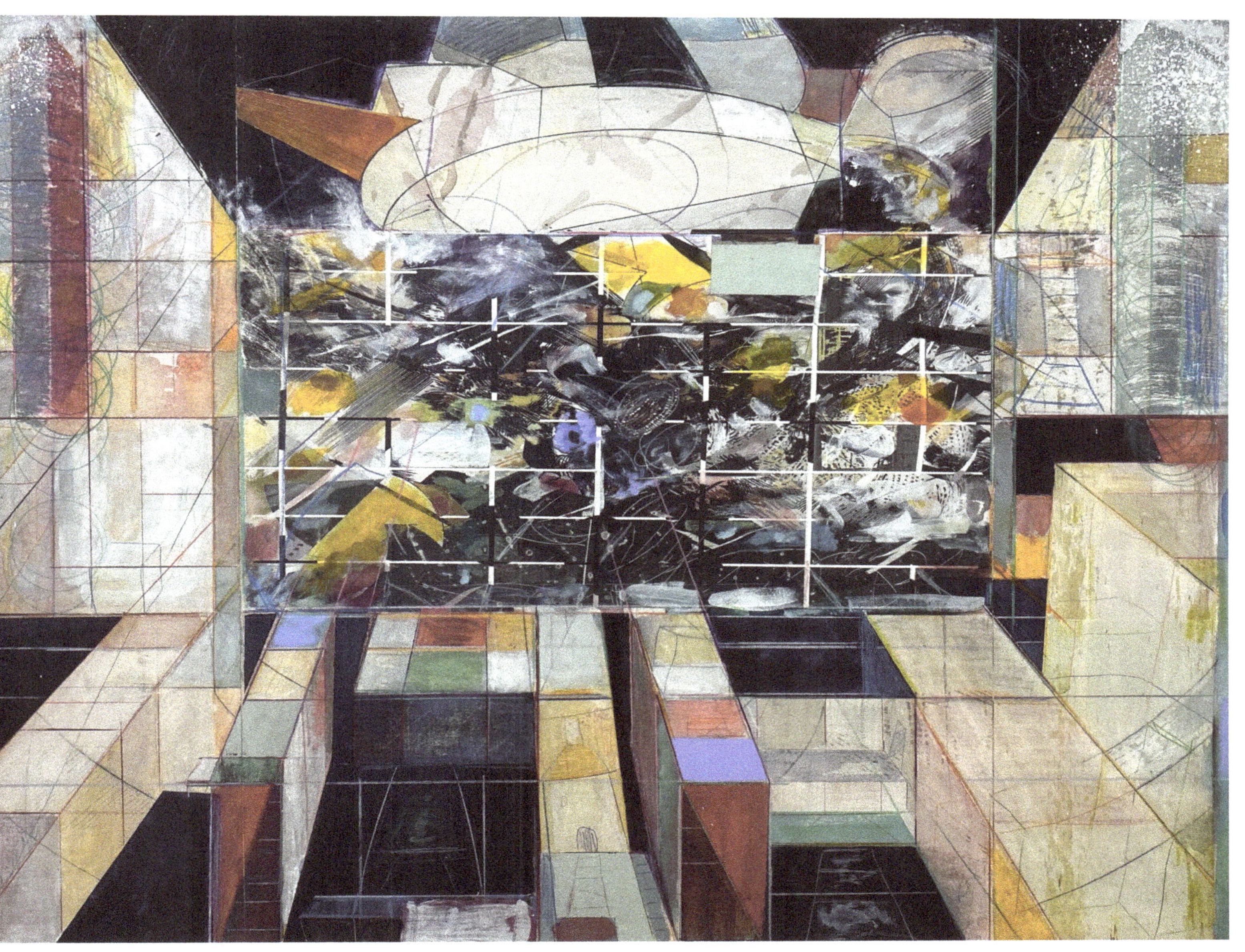

Vital Junction 6
Birch plywood, mono type digital
collage, paint
40x30"
2019

Knockturn Series

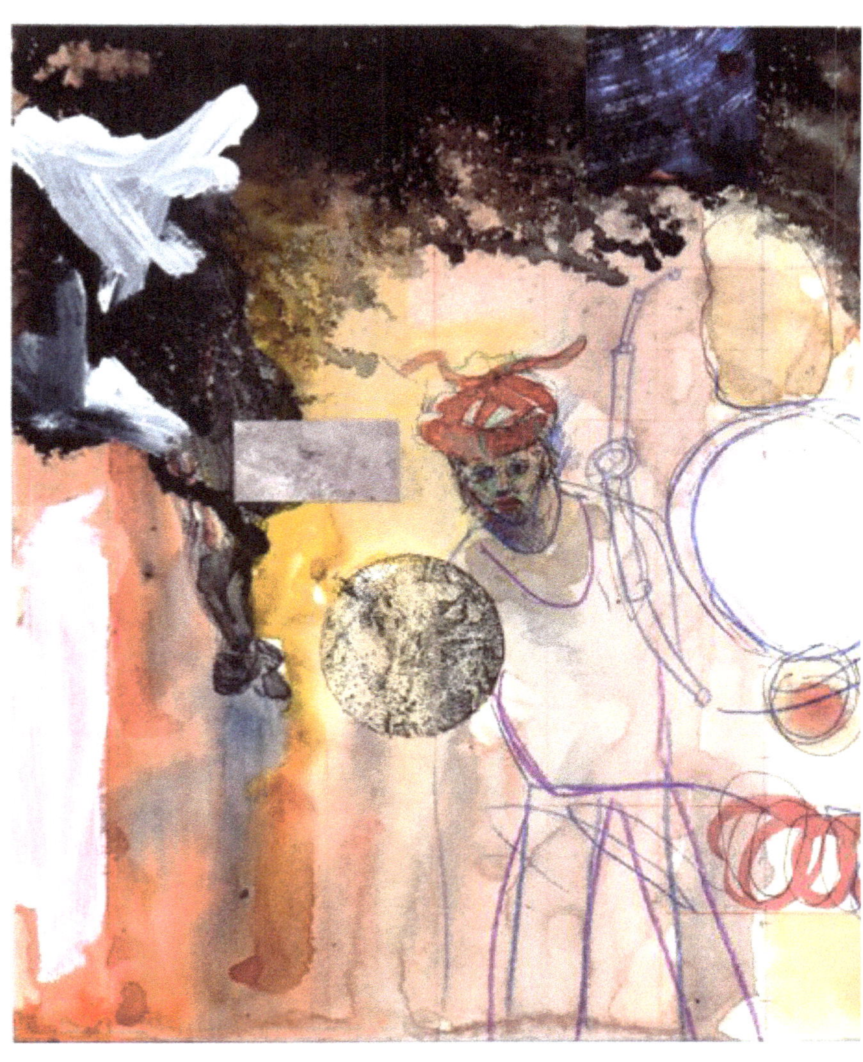

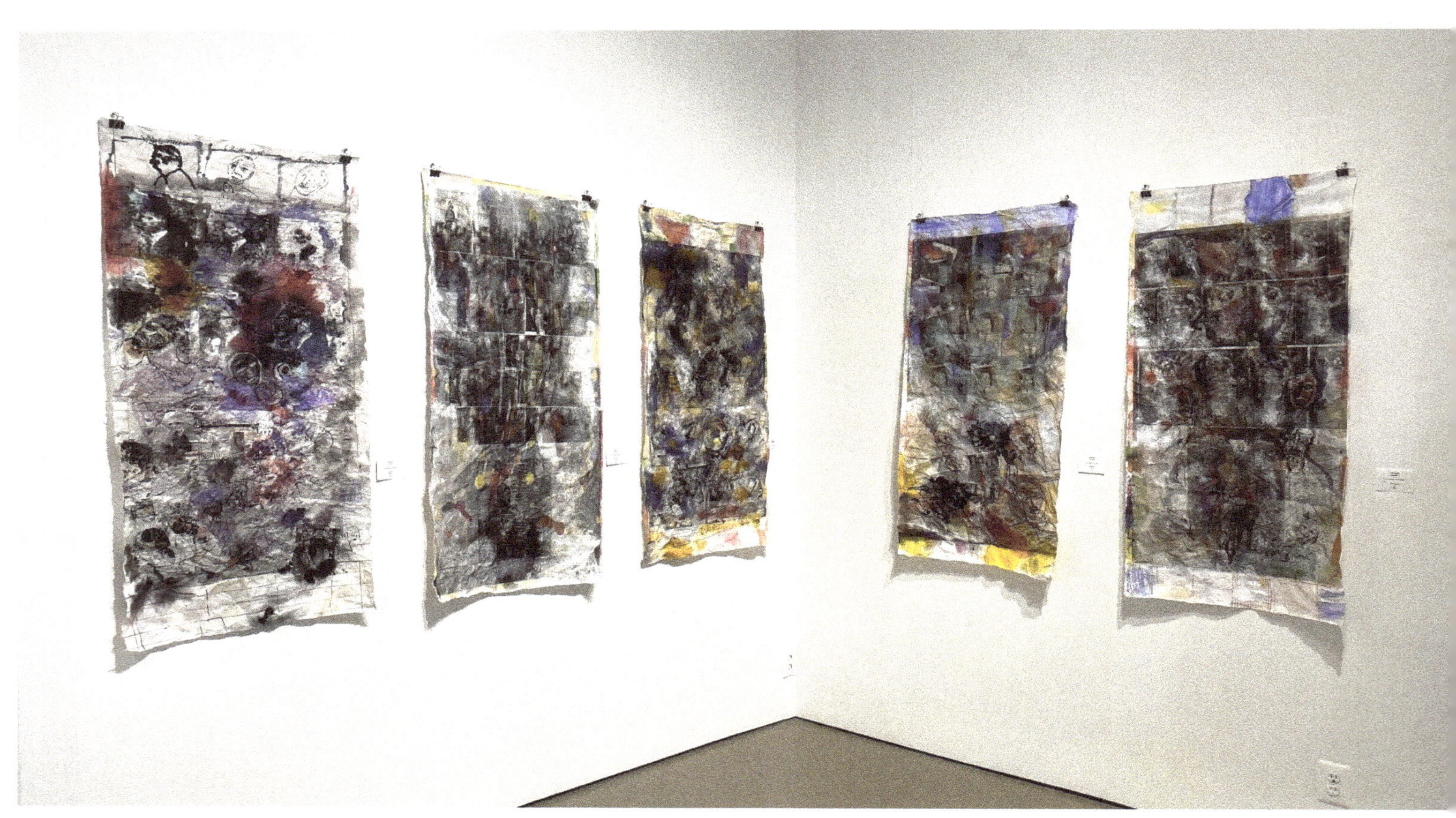

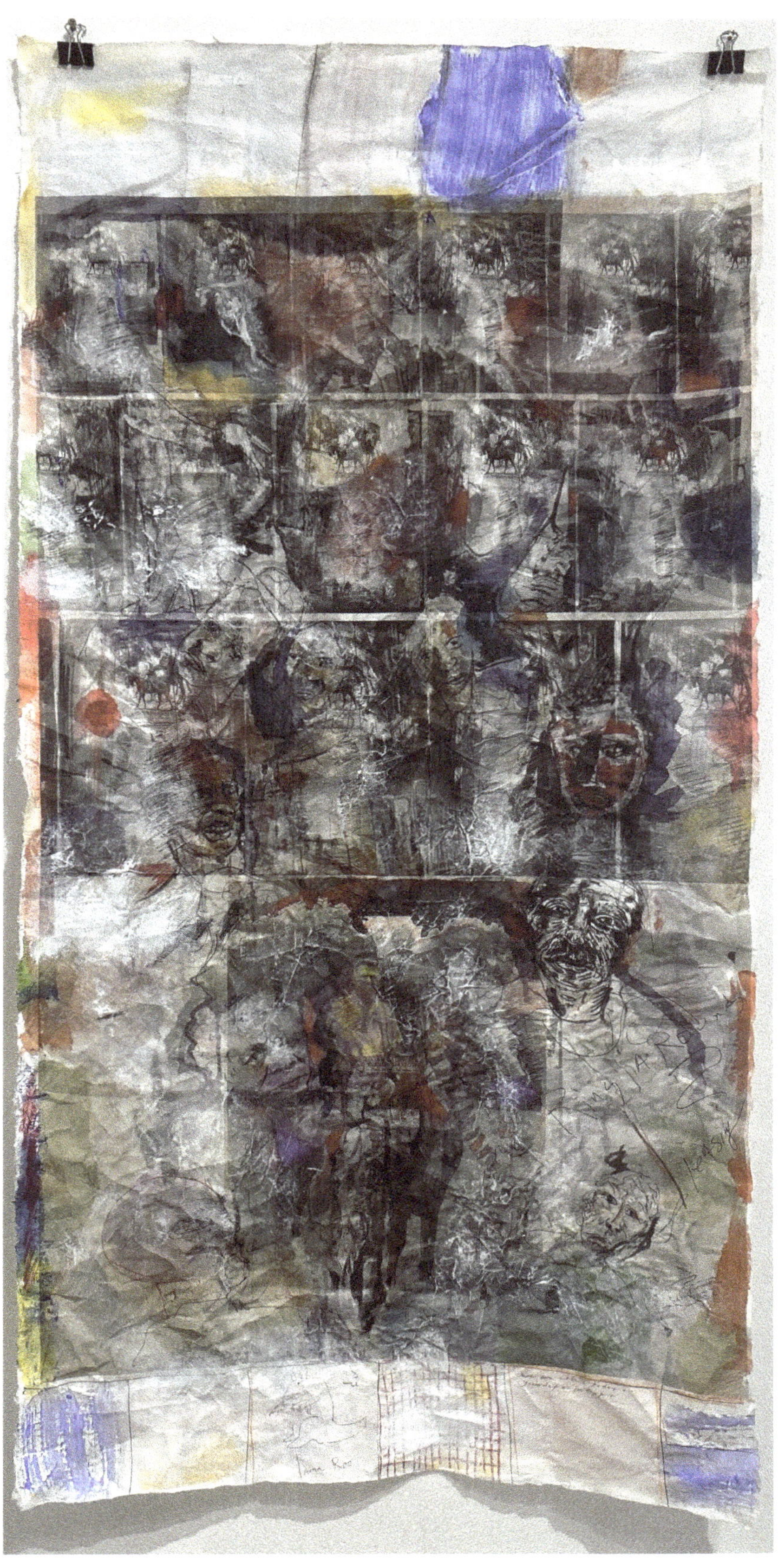

Knockturn 1
Mixed media print and paint
55x28"
2019

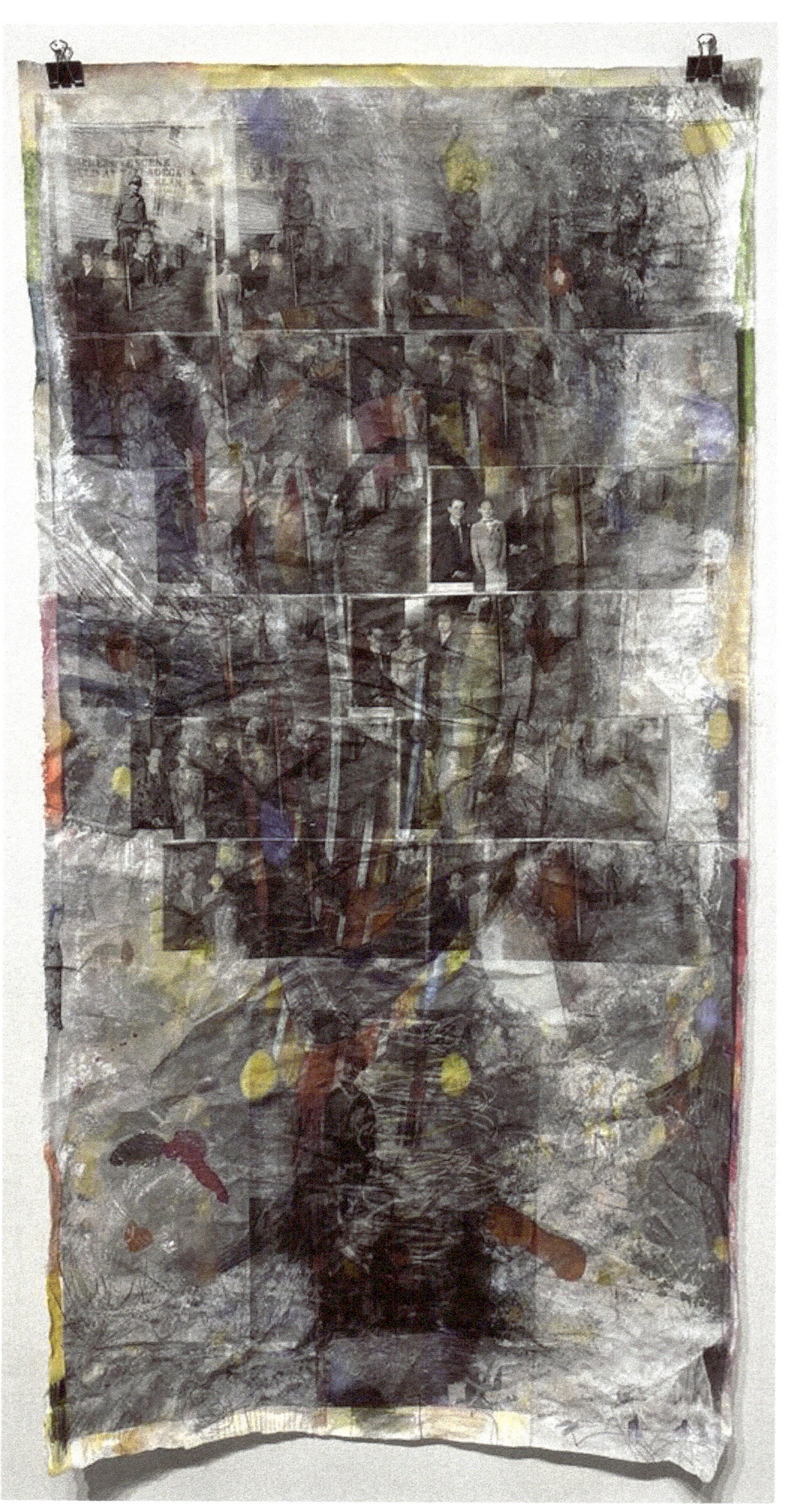

Knockturn 2
Mixed media print and paint
55x28"
2019

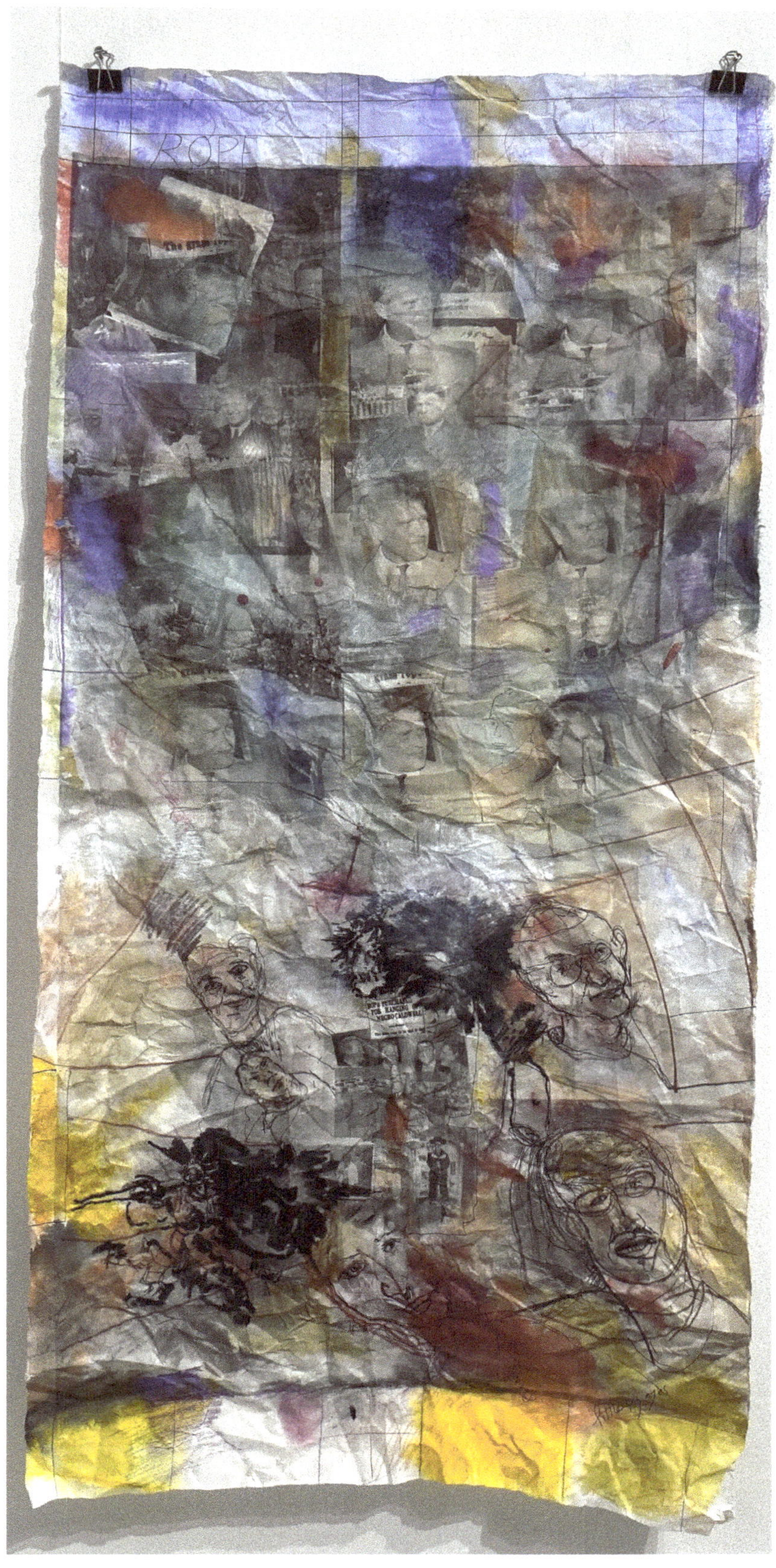

Knockturn 3
Mixed media print and paint
55x28"
2019

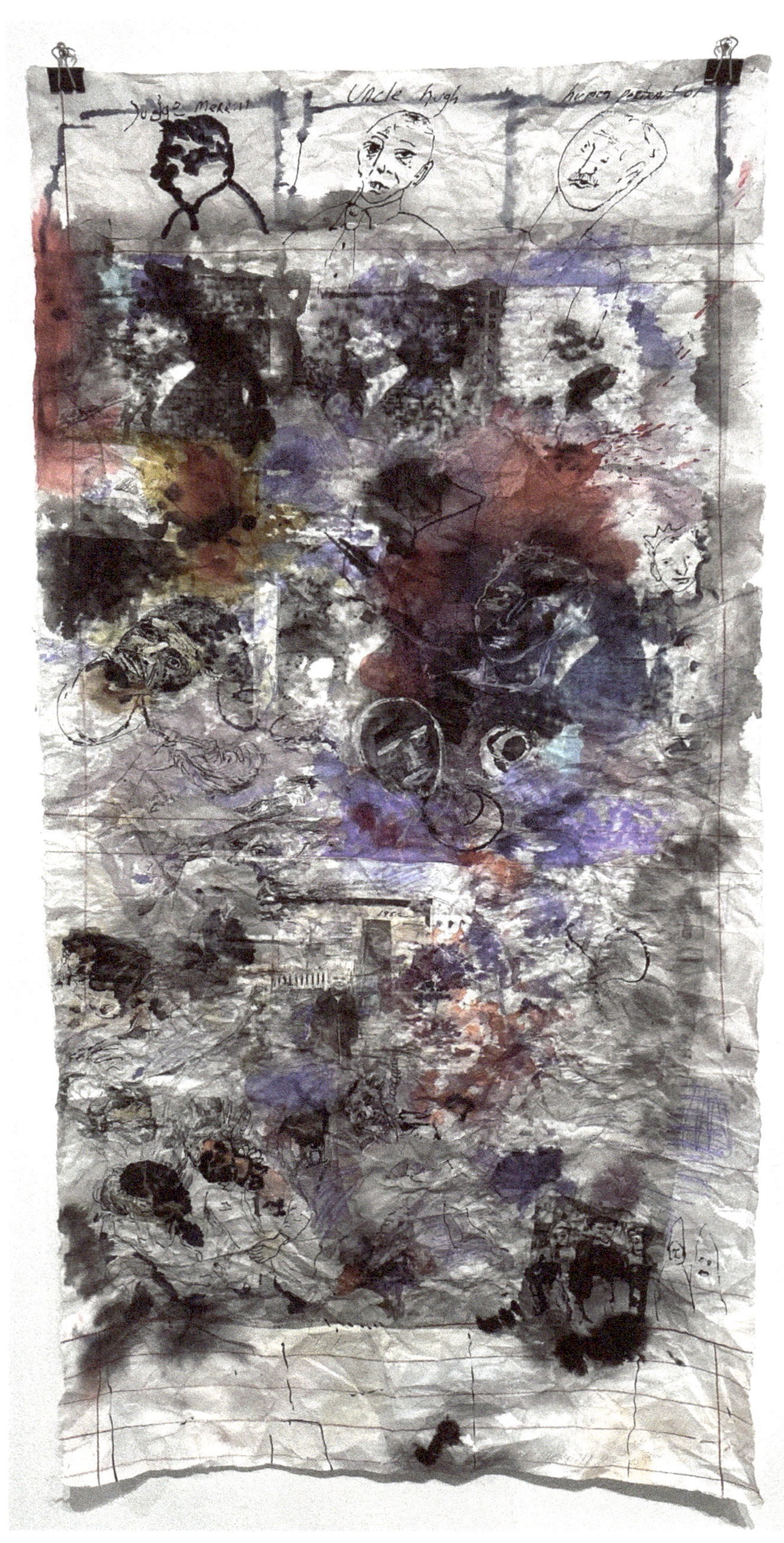

Knockturn 4
Mixed media print and paint
55x28"
2019

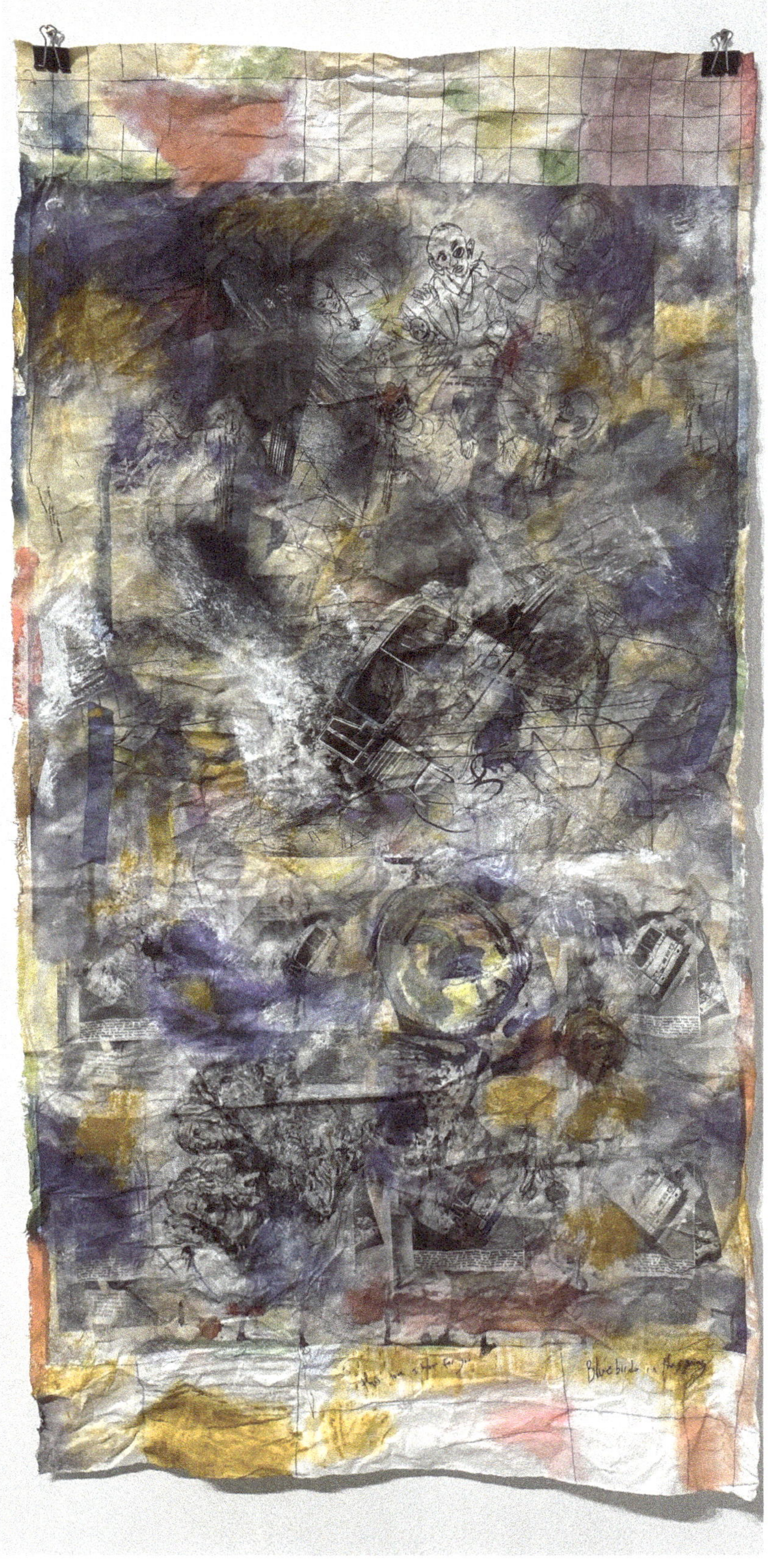

Knockturn 5
Mixed media print and paint
55x28"
2019

Drawing Wall

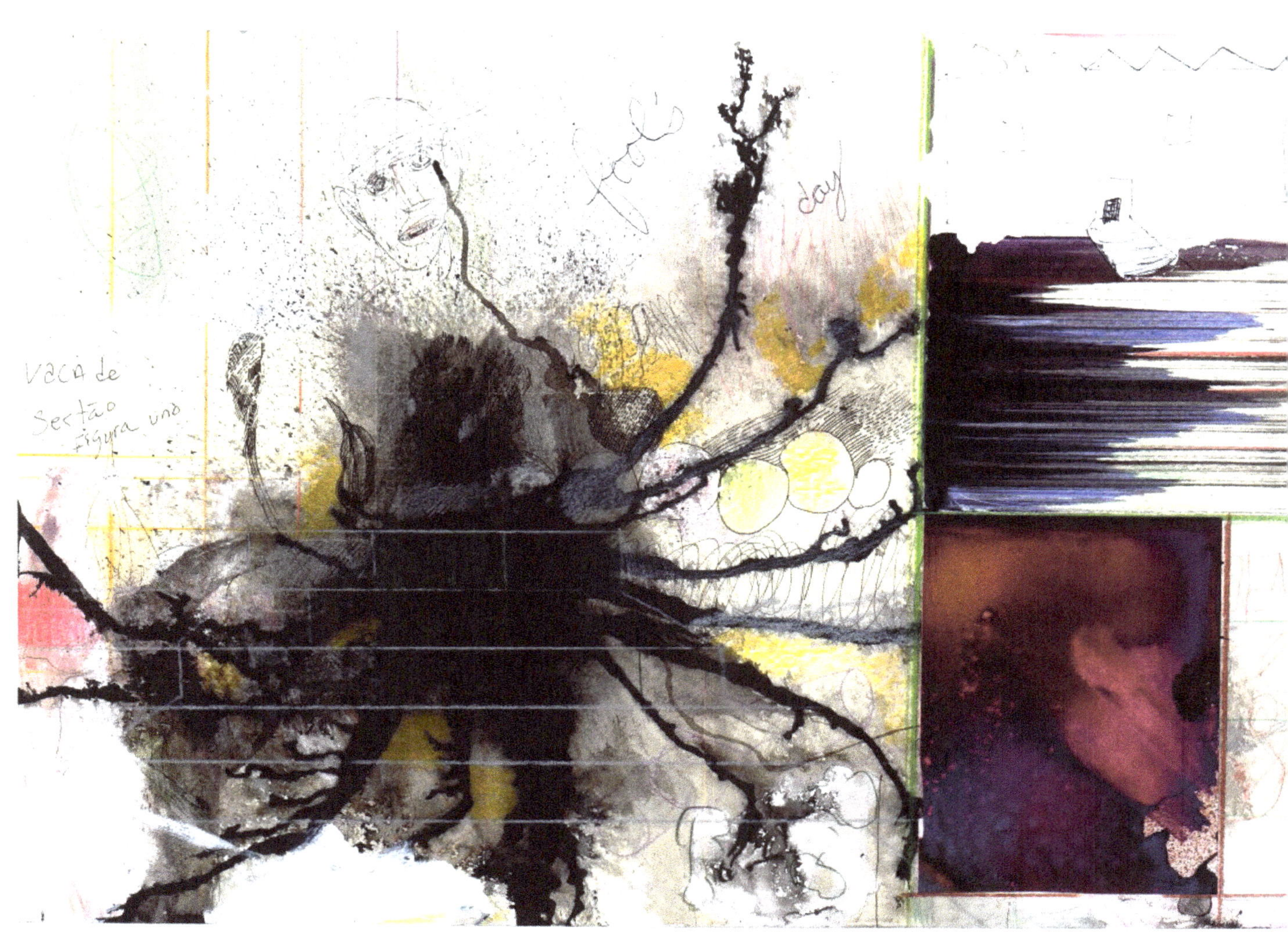

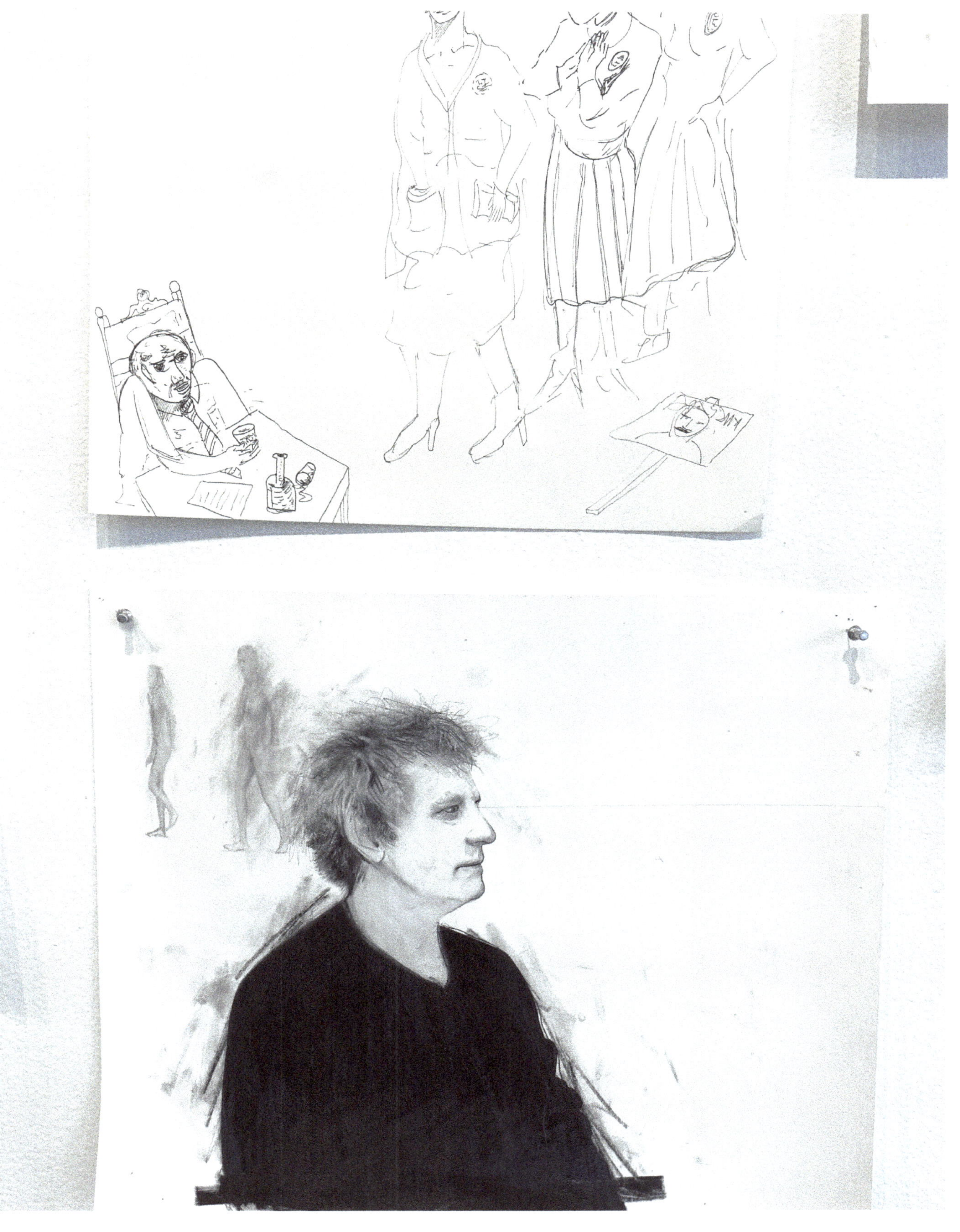

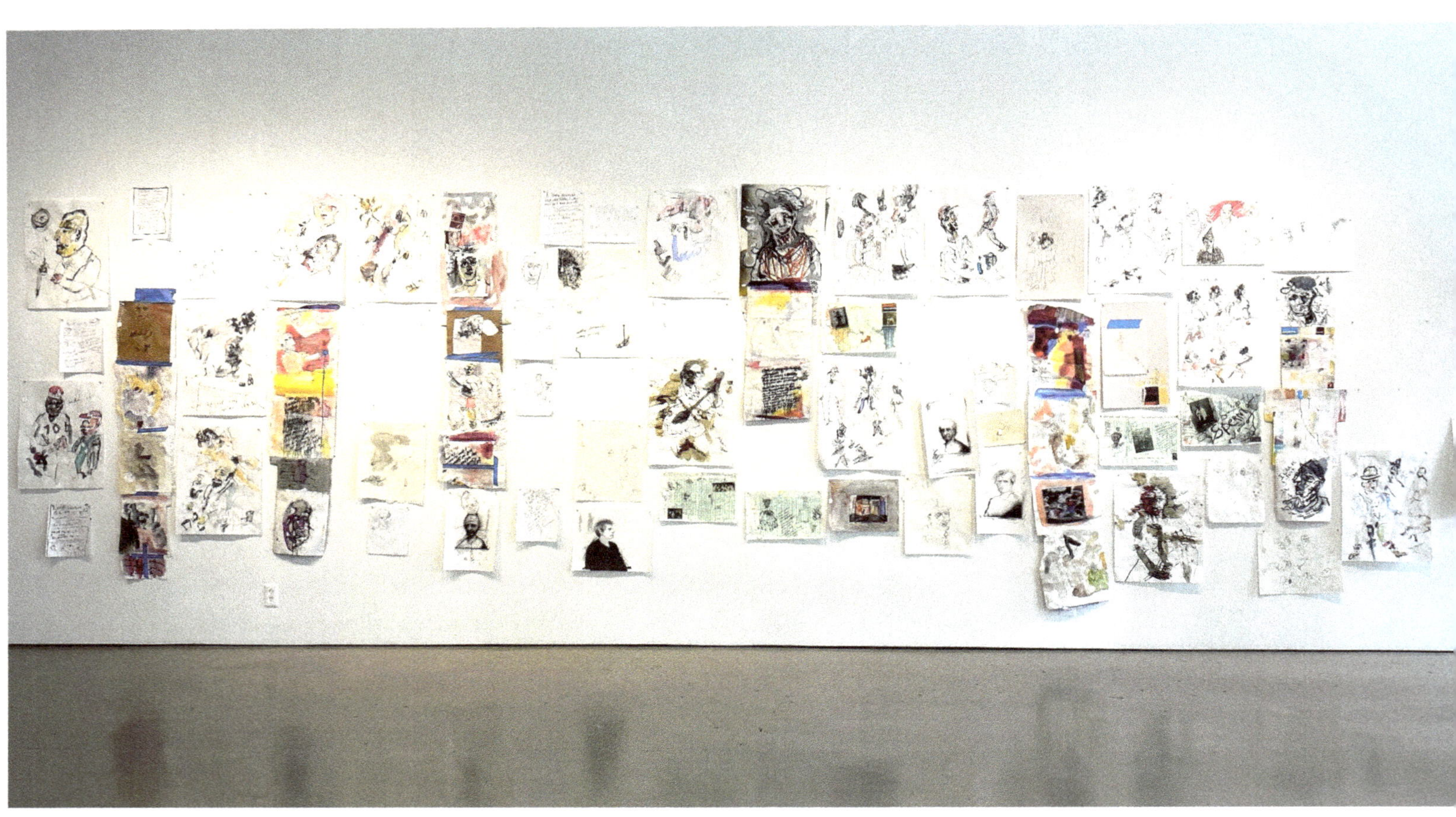

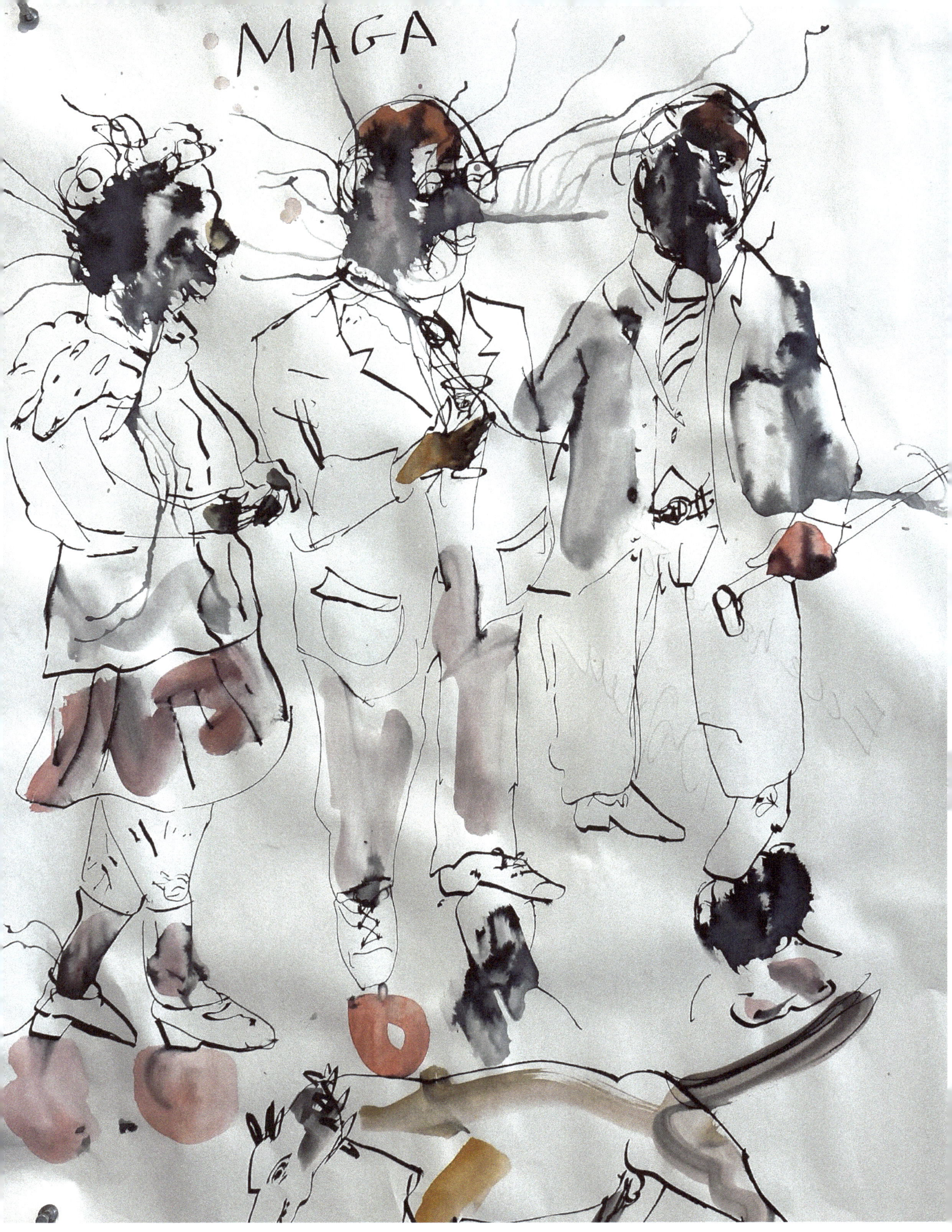
MAGA

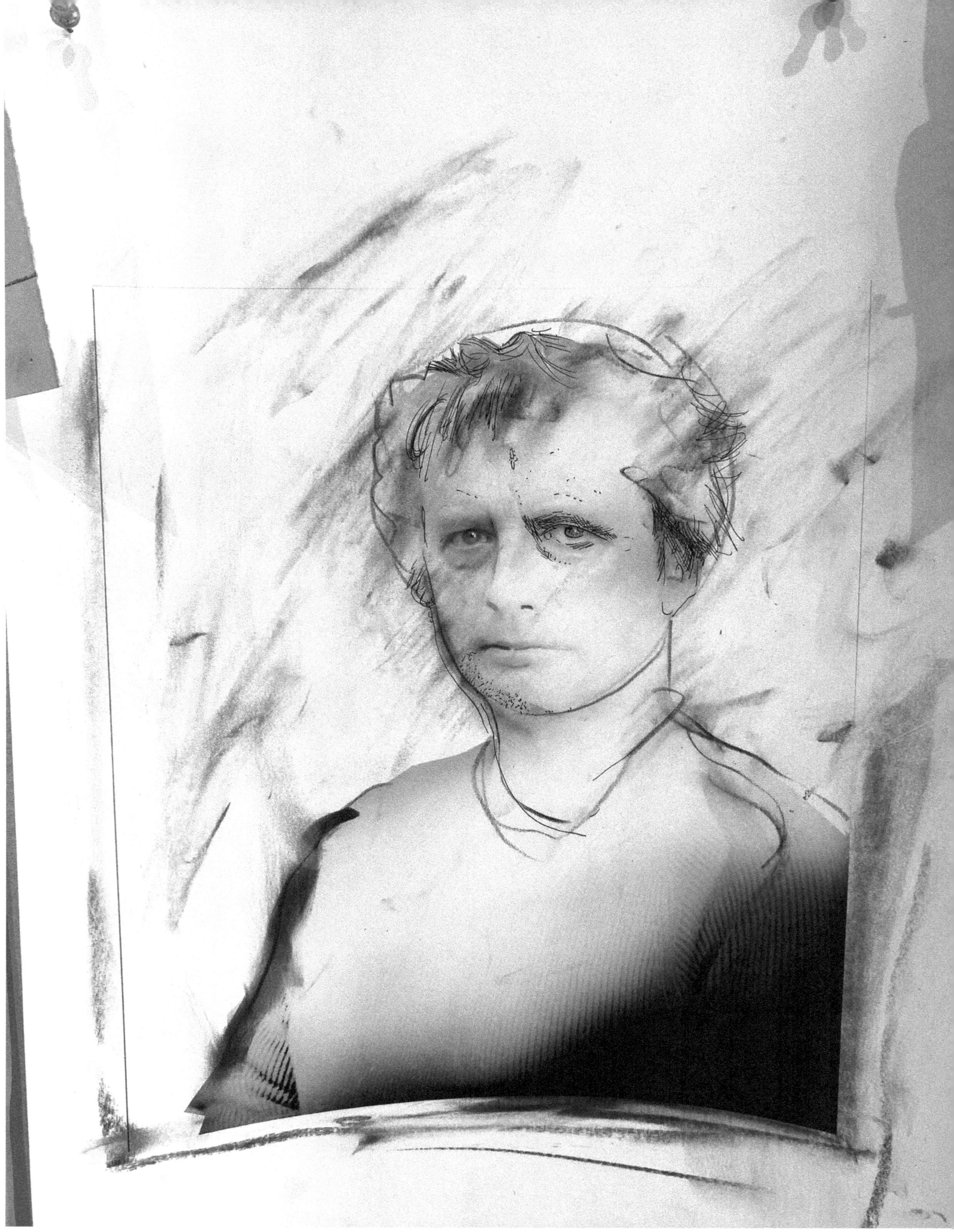

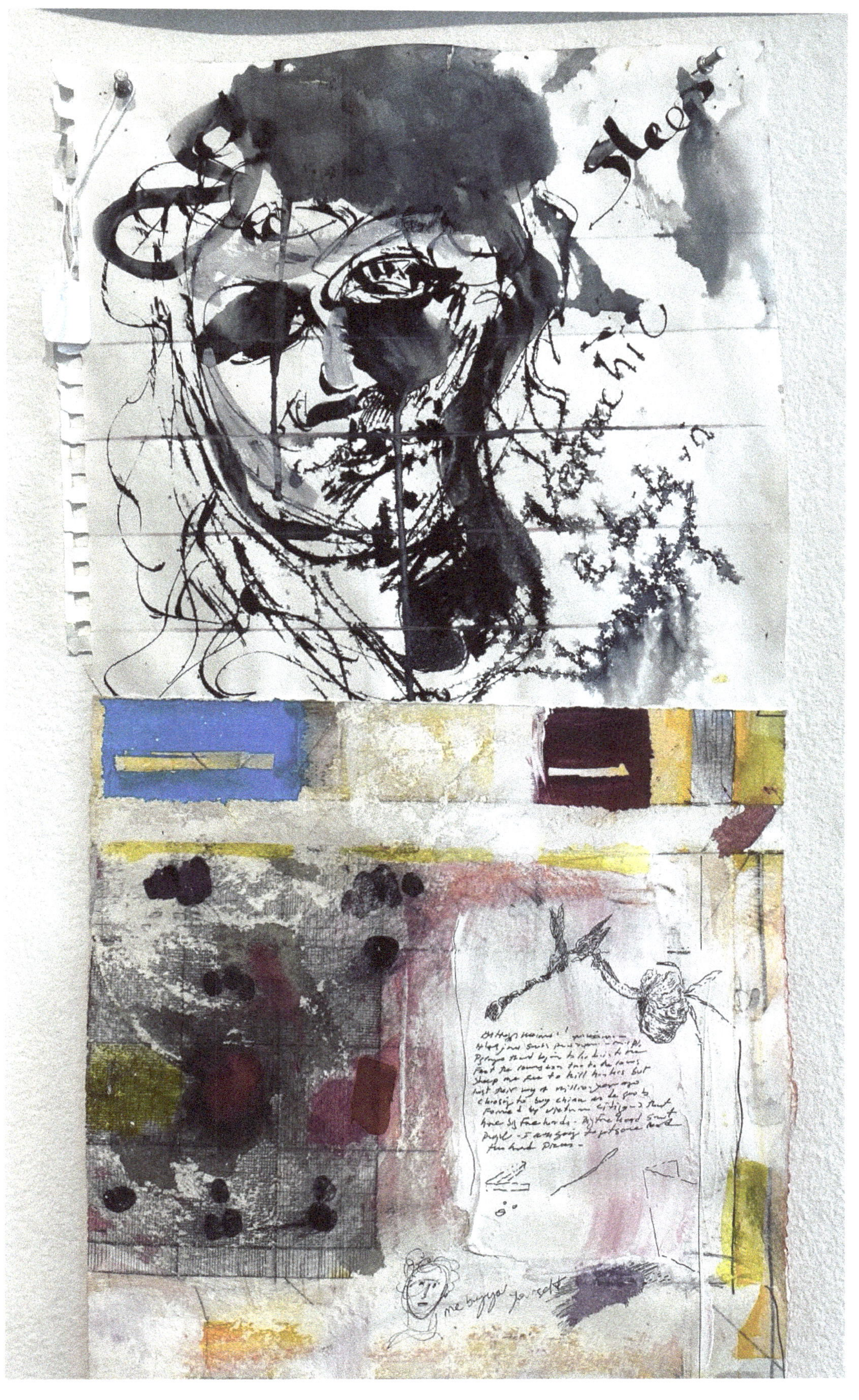

Collaboration: Jeanette & Hugh

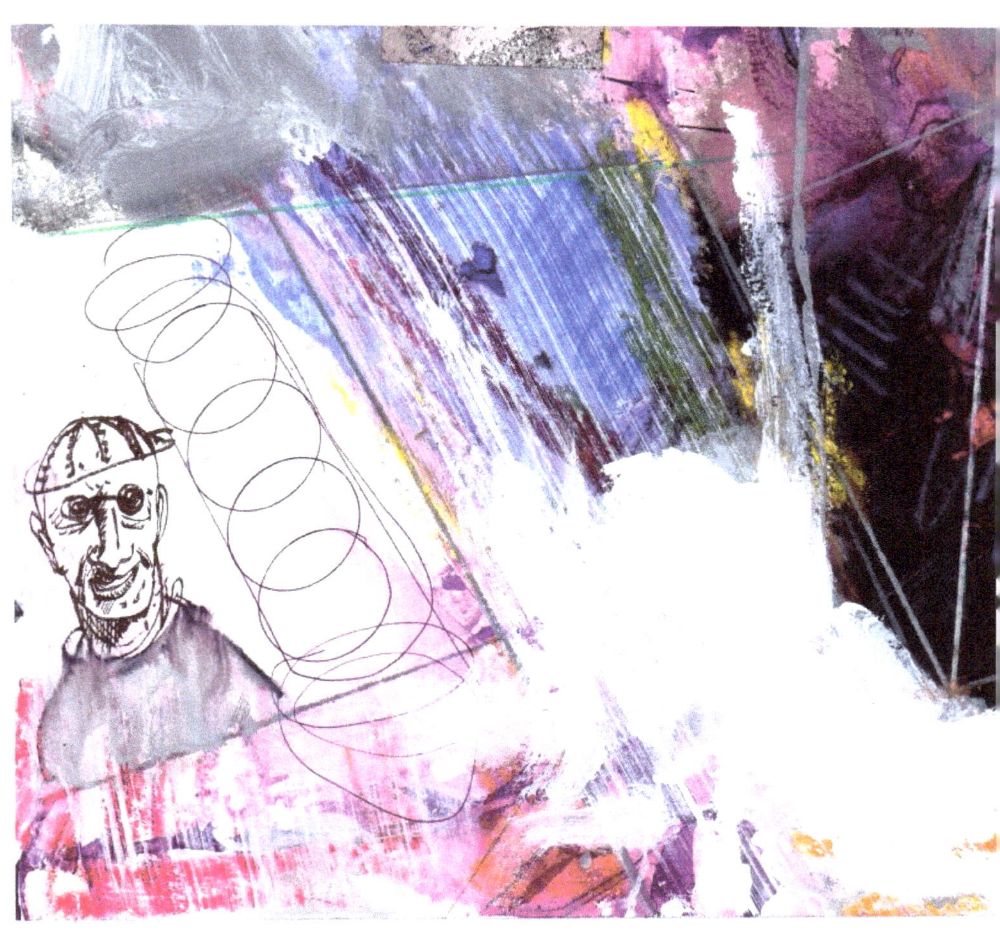

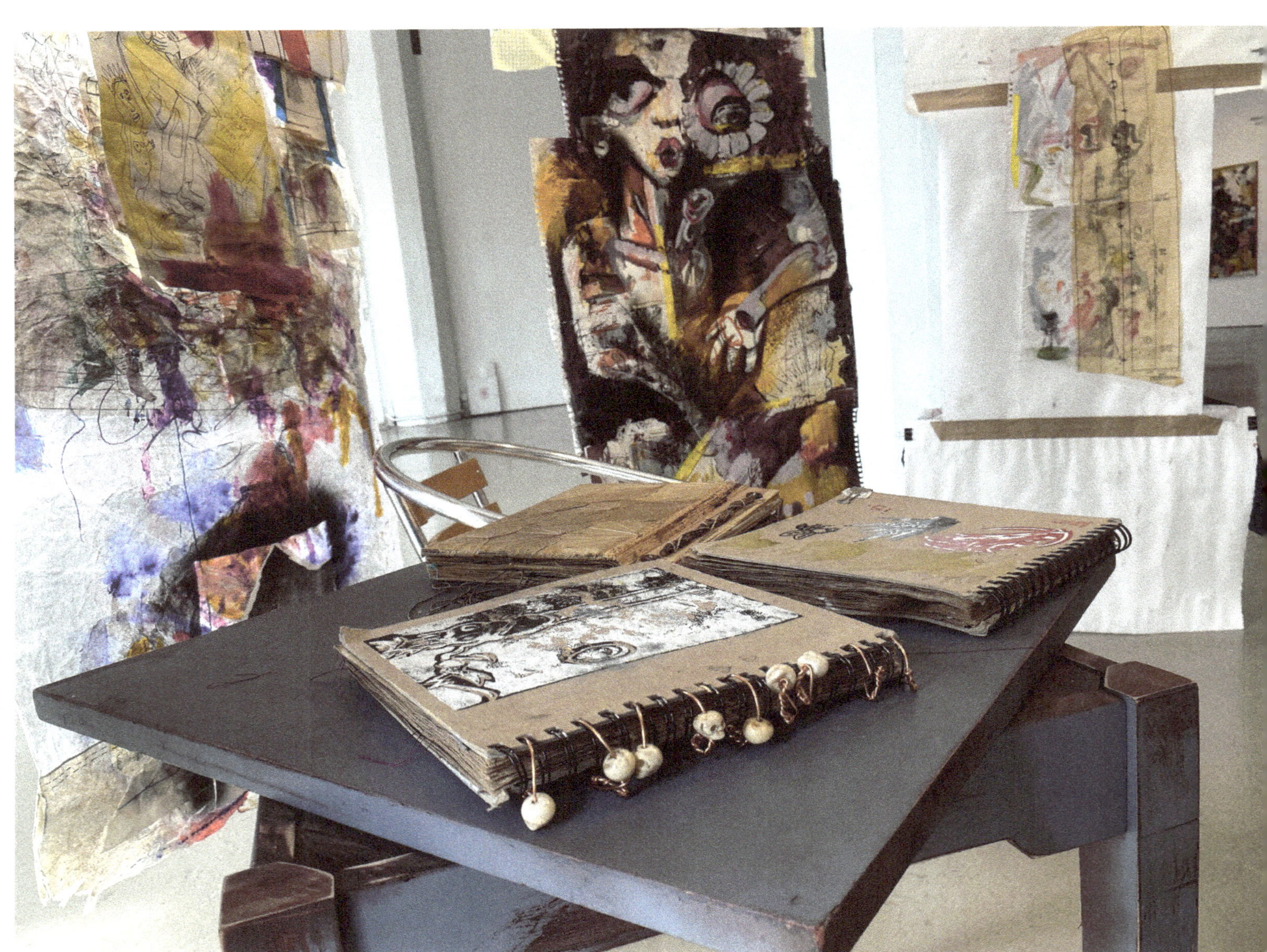

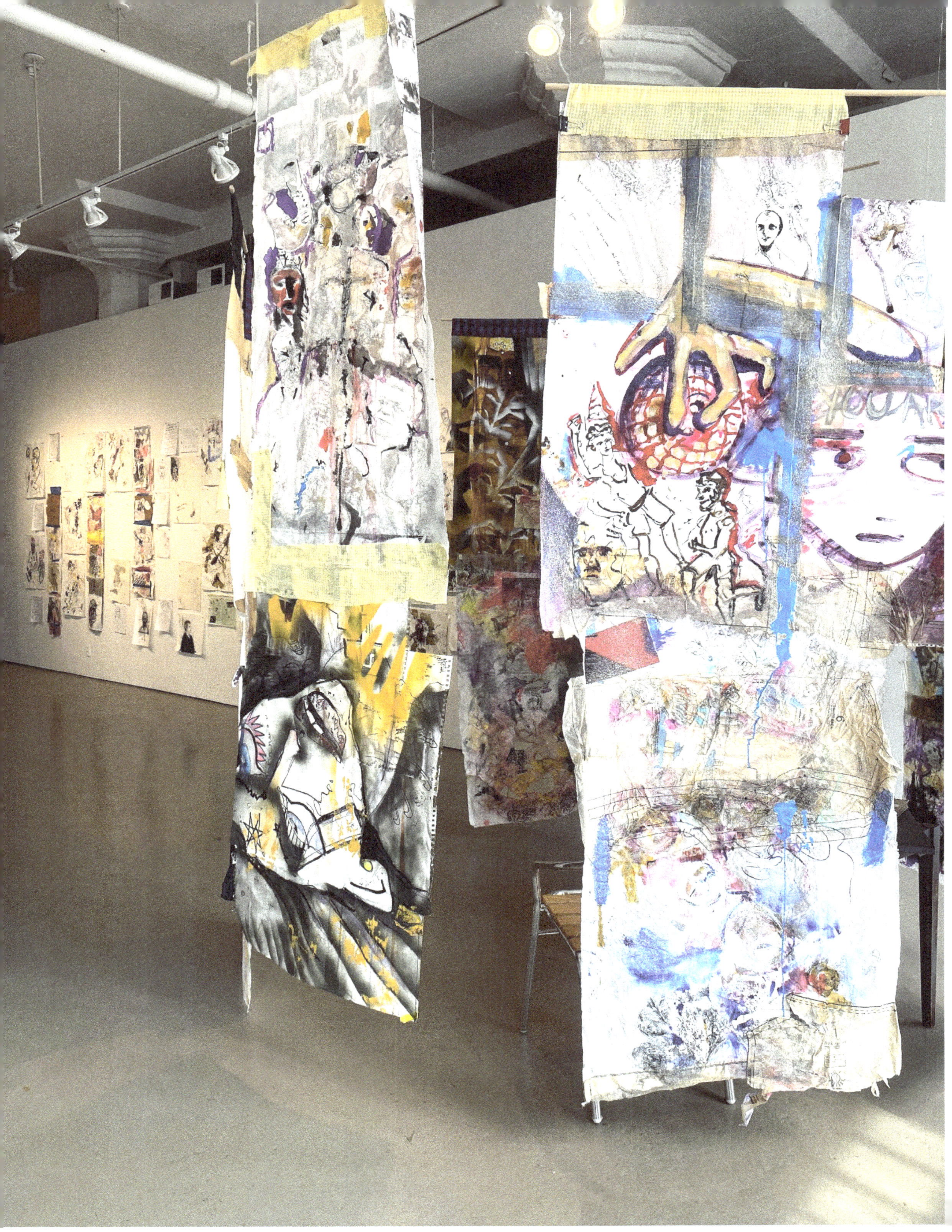

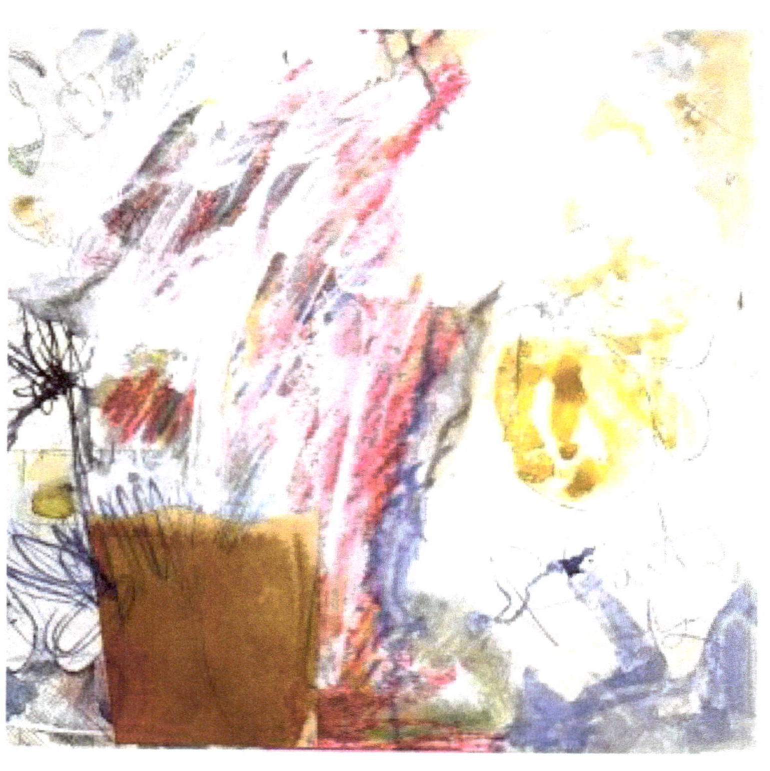